Buckle Down™

Mathematics
Level 3
2nd Edition

This book belongs to: Brooklynn Daiker

Buckle Down
Publishing

Helping your schoolhouse meet the standards of the statehouse™

ISBN 0-7836-4945-2

2BDUS03MM01

1 2 3 4 5 6 7 8 9 10

Senior Editor: Paul Meyers; Project Editor: Lynn Tauro; Editor: Tanya Burken; Production Editor: Jennifer Rapp; Cover Design: Christina Nantz; Cover Graphic Designer: Christina Kroemer; Production Director: Jennifer Booth; Art Director: Chris Wolf; Graphic Designers: Spike Schabacker, Luke Gordon; Composition: Wyndham Books.

Cover image: © Rubberball/Jupiterimages

TABLE OF CONTENTS

Introduction 1

    Test-Taking Tips 2

Unit 1 – Number and Operations 3

    Lesson 1: Whole Numbers 4
        Objectives: N.A.1, N.A.2

    Lesson 2: Computation with Whole Numbers 16
        Objectives: N.A.5, N.B.1, N.B.2, N.B.3, N.C.1, N.C.2

    Lesson 3: Fractions 36
        Objectives: N.A.3, N.A.4, N.C.3, N.C.4

    Lesson 4: Decimals 49
        Objectives: N.A.1, N.C.3, N.C.4

    Lesson 5: Estimation and Problem Solving 60
        Objectives: N.C.5, N.C.6

Unit 2 – Algebra 75

    Lesson 6: Patterns 76
        Objectives: A.A.1, A.A.2, A.A.3, A.C.1

    Lesson 7: Expressions and Number Sentences 89
        Objectives: A.B.1, A.B.2, A.B.3, A.B.4, A.B.5

Unit 3 – Geometry 99

    Lesson 8: Geometric Figures 100
        Objectives: G.A.1, G.A.2, G.A.3, G.A.4, G.A.5, G.A.7, G.D.1

    Lesson 9: Geometric Concepts 118
        Objectives: G.A.5, G.A.6, G.B.1, G.B.2, G.C.1, G.C.2

Unit 4 – Measurement 129

   Lesson 10: Length 130
   Objectives: M.A.1, M.A.2, M.A.3, M.B.1, M.B.2

   Lesson 11: Weight 144
   Objectives: M.A.1, M.A.2, M.A.3, M.B.1, M.B.2

   Lesson 12: Capacity 156
   Objectives: M.A.1, M.A.2, M.A.3, M.B.1, M.B.2

   Lesson 13: Time and Temperature 167
   Objectives: M.A.1, M.A.2, M.A.3, M.B.1

   Lesson 14: Geometric Measurement 178
   Objectives: M.B.3, M.B.4, M.B.5

Unit 5 – Data Analysis and Probability 189

   Lesson 15: Data Analysis 190
   Objectives: D.A.1, D.A.2, D.A.3, D.A.4

   Lesson 16: Probability 210
   Objectives: D.B.1, D.B.2, D.B.3

To the Teacher:

Objective codes are listed for each lesson in the table of contents. The numbers in the shaded gray bar that runs across the tops of the pages in the workbook show the Objectives for a given page (see example to the right). The example below shows what each part of the code stands for.

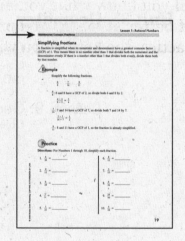

Sample code: N.B.2

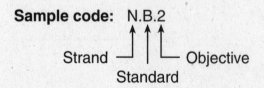

Strand — | | — Objective
Standard

Strands: N = Number and Operations
A = Algebra
G = Geometry
M = Measurement
D = Data Analysis and Probability

Introduction

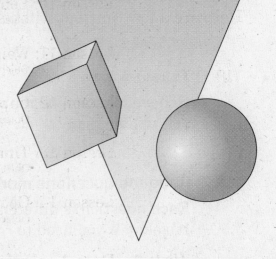

How much math do you know? You probably know a lot—even if it doesn't always seem that way. You have been using math for years. Every year, you add more to what you already know.

Learning to solve math problems is a lot like learning to play a new video game. You need to know what steps to take to stay in the game and come up with the right answers. Math can be a lot of fun if you know what you are doing. How do you get better at math? You practice. The more you practice, the better you will get.

Test-Taking Tips

Here are a few tips that will help you on test day.

TIP 1: Take it easy.

Believe in yourself. You've practiced the problems in *Buckle Down*, so you will be ready to do your best.

TIP 2: Read the questions more than once.

Each question is different. Some questions are tougher than others. It's okay if you need to read a question more than once.

TIP 3: Learn to "plug in" answers to multiple-choice items.

When do you "plug in"? You should "plug in" if your answer is different from all of the answer choices or you can't come up with an answer. Plug each answer choice into the problem and find the one that makes sense. (You can also think of this as "working backwards.")

TIP 4: Answer open-ended items completely.

When you answer an open-ended item, show all your work. Write neatly so that your work is easy to follow. Make sure your answer is clearly marked.

TIP 5: Check your work.

Take the time to check your work on every problem. Checking your work lets you find and fix mistakes you might have made.

TIP 6: Use all the test time.

Work on the test until you are told to stop. If you finish early, go back through the test and double-check your answers.

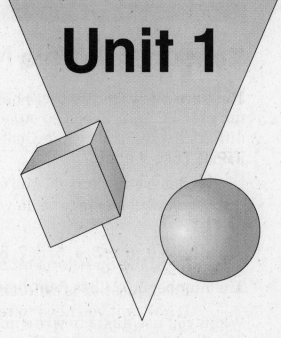

Unit 1

Number and Operations

Numbers are used for just about everything. You might use numbers when you put candles on a birthday cake, keep score at a baseball game, or make a pitcher of juice. You use large numbers to say how far it is from Miami, Florida to Los Angeles, California, or when you write how hot the sun is. You use small numbers to tell the length of an ant or how much a butterfly weighs.

In this unit, you will do all kinds of things with all kinds of numbers—from large numbers like 999,999 to small numbers like $\frac{1}{9}$. You will read, write, compare, order, add, subtract, multiply, and divide numbers. You will work with numbers written as fractions and decimals. Finally, you will learn how to solve story problems.

In This Unit

Whole Numbers

Computation with Whole Numbers

Fractions

Decimals

Estimation and Problem Solving

Lesson 1: Whole Numbers

Numbers are used to describe "how many" of something there are. Some numbers (0, 1, 2, 3, and so on) are known as **whole numbers**. There are different ways of showing whole numbers. You can use digits, words, or models.

Digits

The **digits** 0, 1, 2, 3, 4, 5, 6, 7, 8, and 9 are used to write whole numbers.

The number 1,324 has four digits (1, 3, 2, and 4).

When you use digits to write numbers, you are writing the number in standard form.

> **Standard form:** 1,324

Words

When you use words to write numbers, you write the numbers as you would say them out loud. The following is the word form of 1,324.

> **Word form:** one thousand, three hundred twenty-four

Models

Numbers can be shown using **models**. For example, the following blocks are a model of the number 1,324.

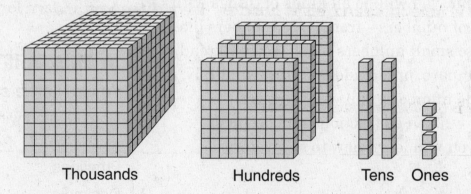

Thousands   Hundreds   Tens   Ones

Practice

Directions: Use the model to answer Numbers 1 and 2.

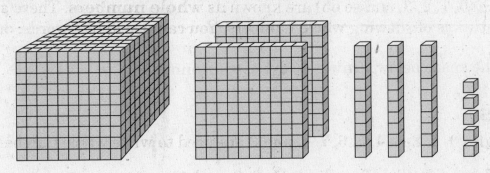

1. How is this number written in standard form? _____

2. How is this number written in words?

   _____

3. How is nine hundred thirty-six thousand, one hundred sixty written in standard form?

   _____

4. How is twenty-four thousand, seven hundred eighty-four written in standard form?

   _____

5. How is nine thousand, eight hundred five written in standard form?

   _____

6. How is 30,008 written in words?

   _____

7. How is 201,579 written in words?

   _____

8. Write a four-digit number. _____ , _____ _____ _____

   Write your number in words.

   _____

   In the space below, draw a model of your number.

9. How is nine hundred eighty-five thousand, six hundred seven written in standard form?

   A. 98,567

   B. 980,567

   C. 985,607

   D. 985,670

10. How is 49,019 written in words?

   A. forty-nine hundred, nineteen

   B. forty-nine thousand, nineteen

   C. forty-nine thousand, one hundred nine

   D. forty-nine thousand, one hundred nineteen

Place Value

Place value helps you understand the value of each digit in a number. The value of each place is 10 times the value of the place to its right.

Ten 1s equal one 10.

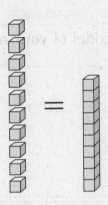

Ten 10s equal one 100.

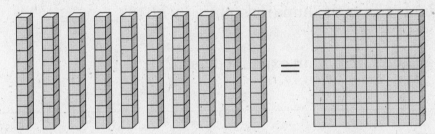

This pattern continues for all places in our number system. Ten 100s equal one 1,000. Ten 1,000s equal one 10,000. Ten 10,000s equal one 100,000.

Example

The following place-value table shows the value of each digit in 739,241.

Hundred Thousands	Ten Thousands	Thousands	Hundreds	Tens	Ones
7	3	9	2	4	1
700,000	30,000	9,000	200	40	1

You can use place value to write numbers in expanded form. The following is the expanded form of 739,241.

Expanded form: 700,000 + 30,000 + 9,000 + 200 + 40 + 1

Practice

1. Write 823,451 in the following place-value table.

Hundred Thousands	Ten Thousands	Thousands	Hundreds	Tens	Ones

How is the number in the table written in expanded form?

_____

2. What number is in the ten thousands place in 52,183? _____

3. What number is in the hundreds place in 7,018? _____

4. How is 492,682 written in expanded form?

_____

5. How is 39,674 written in expanded form?

_____

Directions: Use the following place-value table to answer Numbers 6 and 7.

Hundred Thousands	Ten Thousands	Thousands	Hundreds	Tens	Ones
9	1	7	5	2	8

6. What number is in the thousands place?

A. 1

B. 5

C. 7

D. 9

7. What is the value of the 2?

A.   2

B.   20

C.   200

D. 2,000

Equivalent Representations of Numbers

When you write a number in expanded form, you are **decomposing** the number. When you add numbers together, you are **composing** the numbers. Writing a number in expanded form is not the only way to decompose a number. Most numbers can be decomposed in several ways. Each of these ways is called an **equivalent representation** of the number.

Example

The expanded form of the number 975 is $900 + 70 + 5$.

There are many other ways to decompose the number 975. The following are just three of the many equivalent representations of the number 975.

$$900 + 25 + 25 + 25$$

$$900 + 50 + 20 + 5$$

$$450 + 450 + 25 + 25 + 25$$

Practice

Directions: For Numbers 1 through 3, write three equivalent representations of the given number.

1. 417 _____

   _____

   _____

2. 778 _____

   _____

   _____

3. 1,230 _____

   _____

   _____

Comparing and Ordering Whole Numbers

When you **compare** and **order** numbers, you use the following phrases.

smaller than	the smallest
less than	the least
fewer than	the fewest
greater than	the greatest
larger than	the largest
more than	the most
equal to	the same

Comparing Numbers

You can use the following **symbols** to compare numbers.

$>$ means **is greater than**

$<$ means **is less than**

$=$ means **is equal to**

Think of the symbols $>$ and $<$ as the open mouth of a hungry fish. The fish will **always** swim to the greater number to eat it.

 Example

Compare 10 and 15.

10	$<$	15		15	$>$	10

10 is less than 15.   15 is greater than 10.

You can use a place-value table to help compare numbers.

 Example

How do the numbers 8,235 and 8,214 compare?

Step 1: Write the numbers in a place-value table.

Hundred Thousands	Ten Thousands	Thousands	Hundreds	Tens	Ones
		8	2	3	5
		8	2	1	4

Step 2: Start from the left column and compare the digits until they are different.

Are the numbers in the thousands column the same or different?

They are the same, so look at the numbers in the hundreds column.

Are the numbers in the hundreds column the same or different?

They are the same, so look at the numbers in the tens column.

Are the numbers in the tens column the same or different?

They are different.

Which number has more tens?

$3 > 1$

Therefore, 8,235 has more tens than 8,214.

Step 3: Compare the numbers using symbols.

$8,235 > 8,214$ or $8,214 < 8,235$

8,235 is greater than 8,214 or 8,214 is less than 8,235.

Ordering Numbers

When you order a set of numbers, you write the numbers from **least** to **greatest** or from **greatest** to **least**.

Example

Write these numbers in order from **least** to **greatest**.

23   15   19   18

Compare all the numbers so you are sure to write the least number first and the greatest number last. First compare the tens digits and then the ones digits.

15   18   19   23

Example

Write these numbers in order from **greatest** to **least**.

6,518   5,987   6,027

Compare all the numbers so you are sure to write the greatest number first and the least number last. First compare the thousands digits, then move right, comparing the hundreds digits.

6,518   6,027   5,987

Practice

Directions: For Numbers 1 through 8, use >, <, or = to compare the numbers.

1. 48 _____ 84

2. 472 _____ 472

3. 8,604 _____ 8,460

4. 98 _____ 101

5. 273,429 _____ 285,512

6. 1,682 _____ 938

7. 42,081 _____ 4,890

8. 7,748 _____ 7,739

Directions: Use the information in the following notebook to answer Numbers 9 through 12. Use *is greater than*, *is less than*, or *is equal to* to complete each sentence.

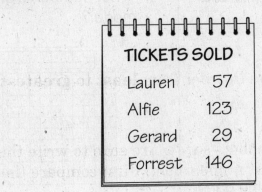

TICKETS SOLD

Lauren	57
Alfie	123
Gerard	29
Forrest	146

9. The number of tickets Lauren sold _____ the number of tickets Gerard sold.

10. The number of tickets Alfie sold _____ the number of tickets Forrest sold.

11. The number of tickets Gerard sold _____ the number of tickets Alfie sold.

12. List the numbers from the notebook in order from **least** to **greatest**.

_____

13. List the numbers below from **greatest** to **least**.

   306,934   360,405   603,504   366,002

_____

14. List the numbers below from **least** to **greatest**.

   53,626   55,023   54,632   53,635

_____

Mathematics Practice

1. How is 9,073 written in expanded form?

   ⓐ 900 + 70 + 3

   ⓑ 900 + 700 + 3

   ⓒ 9,000 + 70 + 3

   ⓓ 9,000 + 700 + 3

2. Which number has a 9 in the ones place?

   ⓐ 1,279

   ⓑ 5,192

   ⓒ 7,951

   ⓓ 9,515

3. Mary Sue has 139 books. Ricky has 147 books. Who has more books than Mary Sue but fewer books than Ricky?

   ⓐ Liz has 142 books.

   ⓑ Eric has 139 books.

   ⓒ Susie has 148 books.

   ⓓ Kelvin has 130 books.

4. What number is shown in the model?

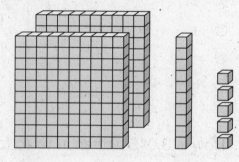

   ⓐ 521

   ⓑ 512

   ⓒ 251

   ⓓ 215

5. Which of the following is an equivalent representation of the number 168?

   ⓐ 100 + 40 + 20 + 6

   ⓑ 50 + 100 + 9 + 9

   ⓒ 40 + 40 + 40 + 8

   ⓓ 50 + 70 + 40 + 18

6. What is the value of the 5 in the number 2,586?

   ⓐ 5,000

   ⓑ 500

   ⓒ 50

   ⓓ 5

7. Which symbol correctly compares the following numbers?

    812,012 _____ 812,142

    Ⓐ >

    Ⓑ +

    Ⓒ =

    Ⓓ <

8. How is 3,015 written in word form?

    Ⓐ three thousand ten fifteen

    Ⓑ three hundred fifteen

    Ⓒ three thousand fifteen

    Ⓓ three hundred one and five

9. The water area in Arkansas is 1,107 square miles. The water area in Oklahoma is 1,224 square miles. The water area in Missouri is 811 square miles. The water area in Louisiana is 8,277 square miles. Which state has the least number of square miles of water area?

    Ⓐ Arkansas

    Ⓑ Oklahoma

    Ⓒ Missouri

    Ⓓ Louisiana

10. The Hudson family has four members. Bobby is 47 years old. Mary is 48 years old. Christina is 14 years old. Carter is 25 years old. Which list shows the order of the Hudson family by their ages from **least** to **greatest**?

    Ⓐ Christina, Carter, Bobby, Mary

    Ⓑ Christina, Mary, Bobby, Carter

    Ⓒ Bobby, Mary, Carter, Christina

    Ⓓ Mary, Bobby, Carter, Christina

11. How is sixty-five thousand, three hundred five written in standard form?

    Ⓐ 6,505

    Ⓑ 6,535

    Ⓒ 65,305

    Ⓓ 65,350

12. Which of the following is **not** an equivalent representation of the number 404?

    Ⓐ 200 + 200 + 2 + 2

    Ⓑ 250 + 150 + 1 + 3

    Ⓒ 300 + 50 + 50 + 4

    Ⓓ 100 + 300 + 4 + 4

Lesson 2: Computation with Whole Numbers

In this lesson, you will add, subtract, multiply, and divide whole numbers. You will also review fact families, factors, multiples, and number properties.

Addition

When you want to find how many of something there are altogether, you **add (+)**. The numbers that you add are **addends**. The answer when you add is the **sum**. The sum is always larger than either of the two addends alone.

Example

Yesterday, Jill saw 7 birds. Today, she saw 3 more birds. How many birds has Jill seen in the last two days?

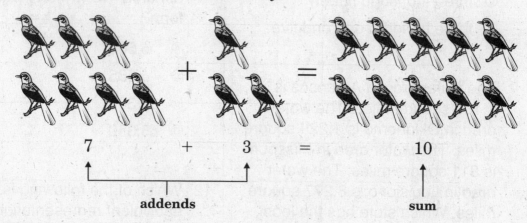

$$7 \qquad + \qquad 3 \qquad = \qquad 10$$

addends   sum

7 + 3 = 10 is an addition number sentence.

Jill has seen 10 birds in the last two days.

When you add numbers, remember that you sometimes need to regroup.

Example

Add: 426 + 398

regroup the hundreds digit → 1 1 ← regroup the tens digit

$$
\begin{array}{r}
426 \\
+\ 398 \\
\hline
824
\end{array}
$$

The sum of 426 and 398 is 824.

Practice

1. Fill in the table with the basic addition facts. Some of the facts have been done for you.

+	0	1	2	3	4	5	6	7	8	9
0										
1								8		
2					7					
3	3									
4		5								
5										
6				9						
7										
8										
9				13						

Directions: Use the following table to answer Numbers 2 and 3.

Maggie's Summer Reading

Month	June	July	August
Number of Pages Read	143	219	126

2. How many pages did Maggie read in June and July combined? _____

3. How many pages did Maggie read in July and August combined? _____

Directions: For Numbers 4 through 15, find the sum.

4. 23
   + 15

5. 19
   + 34

6. 27
   + 55

7. 120
   + 432

8. 358
   + 167

9. 501
   + 510

10. 315
    + 173

11. 294
    + 607

12. 535
    + 453

13. 570
    + 492

14. 242
    + 627

15. 717
    + 191

Subtraction

When you want to take away, find the number left over, or find the difference between two numbers, you **subtract (−)**. The number you take away from is the **minuend**. The number you take away is the **subtrahend**. The answer when you subtract is the **difference**. The difference is always smaller than the minuend.

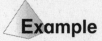 **Example**

This morning, there were 8 hats on the rack in the store. Today, 5 hats have been sold. How many hats are left on the rack?

minuend → $8 - 5 = 3$ ← difference

↑

subtrahend

$8 - 5 = 3$ is a subtraction number sentence.

There are 3 hats left on the rack.

When you subtract numbers, remember that you sometimes need to borrow and regroup.

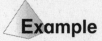 **Example**

Subtract: $319 - 198$

borrow the hundreds digit → 2 11 ← regroup the tens digit

$$\begin{array}{r} 3\cancel{1}9 \\ - 198 \\ \hline 121 \end{array}$$

The difference of 319 and 198 is 121.

➡ **TIP:** The addition fact table on page 17 can also be used to show subtraction facts. For example, to find what $13 - 4$ is equal to, look in the table across the top for 4. Go down the 4-column until you get to 13. Then go across to the number on the left to find that the difference is 9.

Practice

Directions: For Numbers 1 through 10, find the difference.

1.
```
   68
-  17
```

2.
```
   83
-  49
```

3.
```
   97
-  65
```

4.
```
   583
-  141
```

5.
```
   493
-  387
```

6.
```
   704
-  321
```

7.
```
   587
-  423
```

8.
```
   911
-  337
```

9.
```
   696
-  477
```

10.
```
   915
-  706
```

11. Circle the picture that shows a model of 17 − 6.

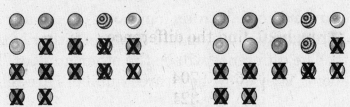 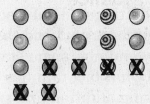

12. Tommy's wagon can carry 50 pounds. He has some toys in his wagon that weigh 34 pounds. How many more pounds can Tommy's wagon carry?

_____

13. There are 17 birds in a tree. If 8 of the birds fly away, how many will be left in the tree?

_____

Directions: The following table shows the total number of cans collected by 3 third-grade classes. Use the table to answer Numbers 14 and 15.

Cans Collected by Third-Grade Students

Class	Mrs. Montgomery	Ms. Sanchez	Mr. Kuhn
Number of Cans Collected	853	972	819

14. How many more cans did Ms. Sanchez's class collect than Mrs. Montgomery's?

A. 115

B. 119

C. 125

D. 129

15. How many more cans did Mrs. Montgomery's class collect than Mr. Kuhn's?

A. 33

B. 34

C. 43

D. 44

Addition and Subtraction Fact Families

Addition and subtraction are **inverse operations** (opposites). Take any two numbers and find their sum. Then take this sum and subtract either of the two numbers you started with. The difference will be the other number. This is what fact families are all about. They show how three numbers are related using addition and subtraction.

Example

Here is the addition and subtraction fact family for the numbers 3, 4, and 7.

addition number sentences	subtraction number sentences
$3 + 4 = 7$	$7 - 4 = 3$
$4 + 3 = 7$	$7 - 3 = 4$

Practice

1. Complete the addition and subtraction fact family.

   addition number sentences   subtraction number sentences

   $5 + 2 = 7$ _____

   _____   _____

2. Complete the addition and subtraction fact family.

   addition number sentences   subtraction number sentences

   _____   _____

   _____ $12 - 9 = 3$

3. What is the addition and subtraction fact family for 2, 6, and 8?

   addition number sentences   subtraction number sentences

   _____   _____

   _____   _____

Multiplication

When you **multiply** (×), you add the same number over and over again. The numbers that you multiply are **factors**. The answer when you multiply is the **product**. The product is always larger than either of the two factors (unless one of the factors is 1).

◢ **Example**

A sandwich is made using 2 slices of bread. How many slices of bread does it take to make 3 sandwiches?

You can solve this problem using **skip counting**. Skip count by the number of slices from each sandwich.

2, 4, 6

You can also solve the problem using **repeated addition**. Add the number of slices from each sandwich.

2 + 2 + 2 = 6

This is how you would solve the problem using multiplication.

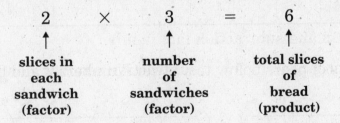

$$2 \qquad \times \qquad 3 \qquad = \qquad 6$$

| slices in each sandwich (factor) | number of sandwiches (factor) | total slices of bread (product) |

2 × 3 = 6 is a multiplication number sentence.

It takes 6 slices of bread to make 3 sandwiches.

 TIP: Skip counting is sometimes called **counting by multiples**. You will read about multiples later in this lesson.

Practice

1. Fill in the table with the basic multiplication facts. Some of the facts have been done for you.

×	1	2	3	4	5	6	7	8	9	10
1										
2			6							
3										
4										
5	5									
6							42			
7										
8										
9				36						90
10										

Directions: Use the sets of pears below to answer Numbers 2 and 3.

2. Use repeated addition to find the total number of pears.

_____

3. Use multiplication to find the total number of pears.

_____ × _____ = _____

Directions: Use the hammers below to answer Numbers 4 through 6.

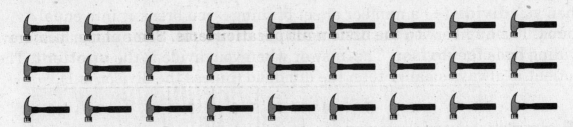

4. Use repeated addition to find the total number of hammers.

   _____

5. Use skip counting to find the total number of hammers.

   _____

6. Use multiplication to find the total number of hammers.

   _____ × _____ = _____

7. Which number sentence represents the total number of peas?

   A. $5 \times 6 = 30$
   B. $5 \times 5 = 25$
   C. $4 \times 4 = 16$
   D. $6 \times 4 = 24$

8. McKenzie has 4 groups of 3 dolls. Which number sentence represents the total number of dolls McKenzie has?

   A. $3 \times 3 = 9$
   B. $4 \times 3 = 12$
   C. $4 \times 4 = 16$
   D. $4 \times 5 = 20$

Division

When you **divide** (÷) a number or set of things, you break it into equal groups. The number you are dividing is the **dividend**. The number you are dividing by is the **divisor**. The answer when you divide is the **quotient**. The quotient is always smaller than the dividend (unless the divisor is 1).

Example

Mr. Morrison gave 12 gold stars to some students. He gave each student 4 gold stars. How many students did Mr. Morrison give gold stars to?

You can solve this problem using **grouping**. Each student received 4 gold stars, so put the 12 gold stars into groups of 4.

There are 3 groups of 4 gold stars.

You can also solve the problem using **repeated subtraction**. Start with the total number of gold stars that were given to the students. Then subtract the number of gold stars that each student received. Repeat the subtraction until you cannot subtract anymore. Count the number of times you subtracted.

$12 - 4 = 8$ (1 time)

$8 - 4 = 4$ (2 times)

$4 - 4 = 0$ (3 times)

You subtracted 4 from 12 a total of 3 times.

This is how you would solve the problem using division.

12	÷	4	=	3
↑		↑		↑
total number of gold stars (dividend)		number of gold stars for each student (divisor)		number of students (quotient)

$12 ÷ 4 = 3$ is a division number sentence.

Mr. Morrison gave the 12 gold stars to 3 students.

Practice

1. There are 8 friends riding the cars at the amusement park. There are 2 friends in each car.

   How many cars are needed for all 8 friends? _____

   Write a division number sentence: _____ ÷ _____ = _____

2. Javier uses 4 lemons to make a glass of lemonade. How many glasses of lemonade can Javier make with the following 28 lemons? Use grouping to solve the problem.

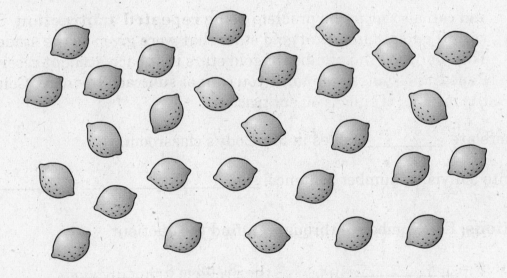

   Javier can make _____ glasses of lemonade.

   Write a division number sentence: _____ ÷ _____ = _____

3. There are 24 students in Mr. Cody's class. There are 6 students sitting at each table. How many tables are there in Mr. Cody's classroom? Use repeated subtraction in the space below to solve the problem.

There are _____ tables in Mr. Cody's classroom.

Write a division number sentence: _____ ÷ _____ = _____

Directions: For Numbers 4 through 11, find the quotient.

4. $35 \div 5 =$ _____

5. $54 \div 6 =$ _____

6. $72 \div 9 =$ _____

7. $21 \div 3 =$ _____

8. $32 \div 8 =$ _____

9. $63 \div 7 =$ _____

10. $28 \div 4 =$ _____

11. $18 \div 2 =$ _____

Multiplication and Division Fact Families

Earlier in this lesson, you learned about addition and subtraction fact families. There are also multiplication and division fact families. Multiplication and division are also inverse operations. Take any two numbers and find their product. Then take this product and divide it by either of the two numbers. The quotient will be the other number. These two math problems will be in the same fact family.

Example

Here is the multiplication and division fact family for the numbers 6, 8, and 48.

multiplication number sentences	division number sentences
$6 \times 8 = 48$	$48 \div 8 = 6$
$8 \times 6 = 48$	$48 \div 6 = 8$

Practice

1. Complete the following multiplication and division fact family.

   multiplication number sentences   division number sentences

   $4 \times 9 = 36$ _____

   _____   _____

2. Complete the following multiplication and division fact family.

   multiplication number sentences   division number sentences

   _____   _____

   _____ $10 \div 2 = 5$

3. What is the multiplication and division fact family for 1, 7, and 7?

   multiplication number sentences   division number sentences

   _____   _____

   _____   _____

Factors

Factors of a whole number are two whole numbers that are multiplied to give the desired product. Factors always come in pairs.

 Example

What are the factors of 12?

$$1 \times 12 = 12$$

$$2 \times 6 = 12$$

$$3 \times 4 = 12$$

The pairs of factors of 12 are 1 and 12, 2 and 6, and 3 and 4.

The factors of 12 are 1, 2, 3, 4, 6, and 12.

Practice

Directions: For Numbers 1 through 3, list the factors of the given number.

1. 9 _____

2. 10 _____

3. 24 _____

4. Which is a pair of factors of 15?

A. 3 and 5

B. 4 and 4

C. 6 and 2

D. 7 and 8

5. Which number does **not** have 4 as a factor?

A. 8

B. 10

C. 16

D. 24

Multiples

A **multiple** of a whole number is found by multiplying that number by any other whole number.

Example

What are the multiples of 3?

$3 \times 0 = \mathbf{0}$ $3 \times 5 = \mathbf{15}$

$3 \times 1 = \mathbf{3}$ $3 \times 6 = \mathbf{18}$

$3 \times 2 = \mathbf{6}$ $3 \times 7 = \mathbf{21}$

$3 \times 3 = \mathbf{9}$ $3 \times 8 = \mathbf{24}$

$3 \times 4 = \mathbf{12}$ and so on . . .

The first nine multiples of 3 are 0, 3, 6, 9, 12, 15, 18, 21, and 24.

Practice

1. List the first 12 multiples of 2. _____

2. List the first 3 multiples of 7. _____

3. List the first 6 multiples of 4. _____

4. List the first 5 multiples of 5. _____

5. Which number is a multiple of 8?

   A. 12

   B. 16

   C. 18

   D. 22

6. Which number is **not** a multiple of 9?

   A. 3

   B. 9

   C. 36

   D. 54

Whole Number Properties

Number properties are rules that help us understand and work with numbers.

Commutative Property of Addition

This rule states that the **order** in which you add two numbers **does not change the sum**.

$$4 + 2 = 2 + 4$$
$$6 = 6$$

Associative Property of Addition

This rule states that when you **add three numbers** it doesn't matter **which two you add first**. Parentheses ( ) can be used to show which two numbers you add first.

$$(3 + 6) + 7 = 3 + (6 + 7)$$
$$9 \ + 7 = 3 + \ 13$$
$$16 = 16$$

Commutative Property of Multiplication

This rule states that the **order** of the factors **does not change the product**.

$$7 \times 4 = 4 \times 7$$
$$28 = 28$$

Associative Property of Multiplication

This rule states that when you **multiply three numbers**, it doesn't matter **which two you multiply first**. Parentheses can be used to show which two numbers you multiply first.

$$(2 \times 5) \times 3 = 2 \times (5 \times 3)$$
$$10 \ \times 3 = 2 \times \ 15$$
$$30 = 30$$

 **Practice**

Directions: For Numbers 1 through 4, use the commutative and associative properties of addition and multiplication to fill in the missing numbers.

1. (8 + _____) + 12 = _____ + (9 + _____)

2. 12 × _____ = 3 × 12

3. 5 × (11 × _____) = (_____ × _____) × 2

4. 7 + _____ = 6 + 7

5. Multiply the following three numbers. Be sure to show your work.

 8 × 5 × 6

6. Add the following three numbers. Be sure to show your work.

 14 + 25 + 15

7. Add the three numbers from Number 6 in a different order. Be sure to show your work.

 Is the answer the same as in Number 6? _____

Mathematics Practice

1. Add: 119 + 387

   Ⓐ 406

   Ⓑ 472

   Ⓒ 496

   Ⓓ 506

2. Which of the following is a factor of 21?

   Ⓐ 4

   Ⓑ 6

   Ⓒ 7

   Ⓓ 9

3. Which is an example of the commutative property of multiplication?

   Ⓐ $4 \times (11 \times 5) = (4 \times 11) \times 5$

   Ⓑ $6 \times 10 = 10 \times 6$

   Ⓒ $3 \times 8 = 12 \times 2$

   Ⓓ $7 \times 1 = 7$

4. What is 5×5?

   Ⓐ 30

   Ⓑ 25

   Ⓒ 20

   Ⓓ 15

5. Which of the following shows the first five multiples of 6?

   Ⓐ 12, 18, 24, 30, 36

   Ⓑ 6, 12, 18, 24, 3

   Ⓒ 6, 9, 12, 15, 18

   Ⓓ 0, 6, 12, 18, 24

6. Subtract: 750 − 687

   Ⓐ 63

   Ⓑ 68

   Ⓒ 163

   Ⓓ 165

7. Which number sentence is in the same fact family as $9 - 2 = 7$?

   Ⓐ $9 \div 3 = 3$

   Ⓑ $9 - 7 = 2$

   Ⓒ $2 \times 7 = 14$

   Ⓓ $9 + 7 = 16$

8. Add: 684 + 217

   Ⓐ 811

   Ⓑ 891

   Ⓒ 901

   Ⓓ 911

9. A toy store had 825 copies of a new video game. The store sold 495 copies in one day. How many copies of the video game does the store have left?

Ⓐ 330

Ⓑ 370

Ⓒ 430

Ⓓ 470

10. Which number does **not** have 64 as a multiple?

Ⓐ 2

Ⓑ 4

Ⓒ 6

Ⓓ 8

11. Which number sentence is in the same fact family as $8 \div 2 = 4$?

Ⓐ $4 \div 2 = 2$

Ⓑ $2 \times 2 = 4$

Ⓒ $4 + 4 = 8$

Ⓓ $8 \div 4 = 2$

12. Which is an example of the associative property of addition?

Ⓐ $7 + 8 = 8 + 7$

Ⓑ $3 \times (2 \times 5) = (3 \times 2) \times 5$

Ⓒ $4 \times 2 = 2 \times 4$

Ⓓ $(1 + 9) + 6 = 1 + (9 + 6)$

13. What subtraction number sentence does the picture show?

Ⓐ $9 + 3 = 12$

Ⓑ $9 - 3 = 6$

Ⓒ $9 - 6 = 3$

Ⓓ $9 - 4 = 5$

14. Multiply:

$$\begin{array}{r} 9 \\ \times\ 6 \\ \hline \end{array}$$

Ⓐ 54

Ⓑ 56

Ⓒ 60

Ⓓ 63

15. What is $56 \div 7$?

Ⓐ 6

Ⓑ 7

Ⓒ 8

Ⓓ 9

16. Which of the following is **not** a factor of 36?

Ⓐ 5

Ⓑ 4

Ⓒ 3

Ⓓ 2

Lesson 3: Fractions

In this lesson, you will use models and number lines to learn about fractions and find equivalent fractions. You will also compare and order fractions. Finally, you will add and subtract fractions with common denominators.

Identifying Fractions

A **fraction** represents a part of a whole or a part of a group. Models, or pictures, can help you understand fractions.

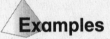Examples

   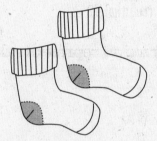

The window is divided into 4 equal parts. $\frac{1}{4}$ of the window is broken. $\frac{3}{4}$ is not broken. In word form, $\frac{1}{4}$ is one fourth; $\frac{3}{4}$ is three fourths.

Each sock is 1 part of a pair. The fraction $\frac{1}{2}$ represents 1 part of the group of 2. In word form, $\frac{1}{2}$ is one half.

The **numerator** of the fraction tells how many parts of the whole or group you have. The numerator is the top number of a fraction. The **denominator** of the fraction tells how many parts the whole or group is divided into. The denominator is the bottom number of a fraction.

$$\text{numerator} \rightarrow \frac{1}{4} \leftarrow \text{denominator}$$

➡ **TIP:** $\dfrac{\text{The n}U\text{merator is }U\text{pstairs.}}{\text{The }D\text{enominator is }D\text{ownstairs.}}$

Practice

Directions: Use the following pictures to answer Numbers 1 through 3.

1. How many sharks are shaded? _____

2. How many sharks are shown in all? _____

3. What fraction represents the number of sharks that are shaded?

_____

4. Color $\frac{3}{8}$ of the following circle.

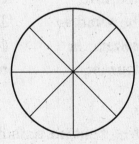

5. Color some of the squares in the rectangle below. Then write the word form of the fraction that represents the colored squares of the rectangle.

_____

Directions: For Numbers 6 through 11, write the fraction that represents the shaded parts of each figure.

6.

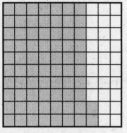

_____

9.

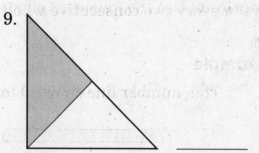

_____

7.

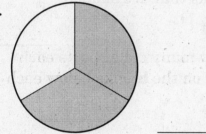

_____

10.

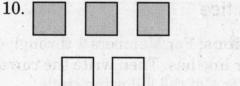

_____

8.

_____

11.

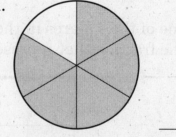

_____

Using Number Lines

Another way to show fractions is by using a number line. Fractions occur between every two consecutive whole numbers.

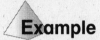 **Example**

This number line shows 0 to 1. It is divided into three equal parts.

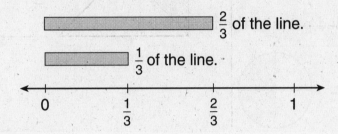

$\frac{2}{3}$ of the line.

$\frac{1}{3}$ of the line.

0    $\frac{1}{3}$ $\frac{2}{3}$ 1

Practice

Directions: For Numbers 1 through 4, count how many equal parts each number line has. Then write the correct fractions on the blanks below each line.

1.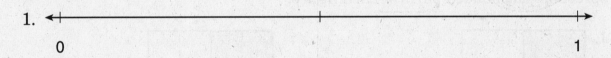

2.

3.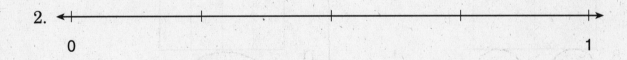

4.

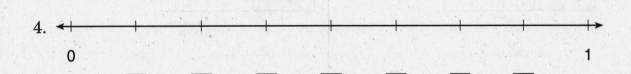

Equivalent Fractions

Two different fractions can represent the same part of a whole. These are called **equivalent fractions**.

xample

The fractions $\frac{1}{2}$ and $\frac{2}{4}$ represent the same part of a whole.

Look at the shaded parts of the two circles.

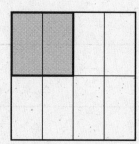

$$\frac{1}{2} \quad = \quad \frac{2}{4}$$

Practice

Directions: For Numbers 1 and 2, write an equivalent fraction that represents the shaded parts of each figure.

1.

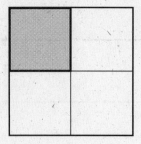

$$\frac{1}{4} \quad = \quad \underline{\hspace{2cm}}$$

2.

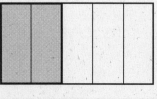

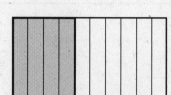

$$\frac{2}{5} \quad = \quad \underline{\hspace{2cm}}$$

Directions: For Numbers 3 and 4, shade an equivalent fraction to the figure on the left. Then write the fractions represented by each figure.

3.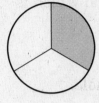

_____ = _____

4.

_____ = _____

5. Write the correct fractions in the spaces below each number line. Then use the number lines to write the fractions that are equivalent to the given fraction.

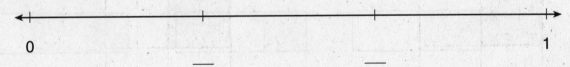

$\frac{1}{3}$ = _____ $\frac{2}{3}$ = _____

Comparing and Ordering Fractions

Models help you see how different fractions compare. As long as the size of the whole is the same, you can tell which fraction is greater and which is smaller just by looking at the models.

 Example

Compare $\frac{1}{3}$ and $\frac{1}{4}$.

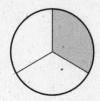

Compare the models.

You can see that $\frac{1}{3}$ is greater than $\frac{1}{4}$.

You can write this as $\frac{1}{3} > \frac{1}{4}$.

 Example

Order $\frac{1}{2}$, $\frac{1}{3}$, and $\frac{3}{4}$ from **least** to **greatest**.

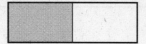  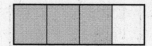

Compare the models.

You can see that $\frac{1}{3}$ is the smallest and $\frac{3}{4}$ is the greatest.

The order from least to greatest is $\frac{1}{3}$, $\frac{1}{2}$, $\frac{3}{4}$.

Practice

Directions: For Numbers 1 through 4, fill in the blanks below each model with the fraction that each model shows. Then write the correct symbol (<, >, or =) on the center blank to compare the fractions.

1.

     _____   _____

2.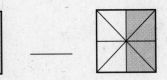

     _____   _____

3.

     _____   _____

4.

     _____   _____

Directions: For Numbers 5 through 7, fill in the blanks with the fraction that each model shows. Then compare and write the fractions in order from **least** to **greatest**.

5.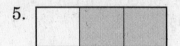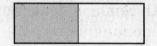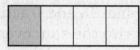

_____   _____   _____

_____

6.

_____   _____   _____

_____

7.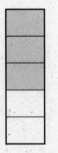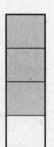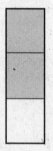

_____   _____   _____

_____

Adding and Subtracting Fractions with Common Denominators

Two fractions have **common denominators** when their denominators are the same. To add fractions with common denominators, add the numerators and write the sum over the denominator.

 Example

Add: $\frac{3}{6} + \frac{2}{6}$

Combine the shaded parts of both circles into one circle.

$$\frac{3}{6} \quad + \quad \frac{2}{6} \quad = \quad \frac{5}{6}$$

Therefore, $\frac{3}{6} + \frac{2}{6} = \frac{5}{6}$.

To subtract fractions with common denominators, subtract the numerators and write the difference over the denominator.

Example

Subtract: $\frac{7}{8} - \frac{3}{8}$

Cross out the shaded parts of the second rectangle from the first rectangle.

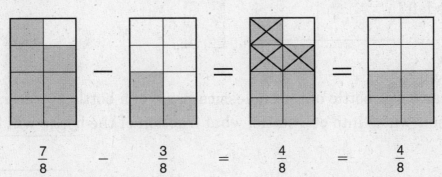

$$\frac{7}{8} \quad - \quad \frac{3}{8} \quad = \quad \frac{4}{8} \quad = \quad \frac{4}{8}$$

Therefore, $\frac{7}{8} - \frac{3}{8} = \frac{4}{8}$.

Practice

Directions: For Numbers 1 and 2, write the fraction for the shaded parts of each figure. Then shade the sum or difference in the blank figure and write the fraction for the sum or difference.

1.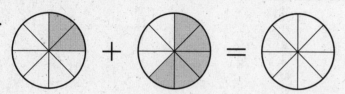

   _____ + _____ = _____

2.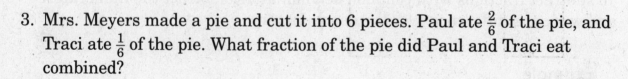

   _____ − _____ = _____

3. Mrs. Meyers made a pie and cut it into 6 pieces. Paul ate $\frac{2}{6}$ of the pie, and Traci ate $\frac{1}{6}$ of the pie. What fraction of the pie did Paul and Traci eat combined?

   _____

4. Lynn ordered a pizza for lunch. She ate $\frac{3}{10}$ of the pizza. How much of the pizza is left?

   _____

5. Scott has $\frac{1}{4}$ of a bottle of water. Jessica has $\frac{2}{4}$ of a bottle of water. If they pour their water into one bottle, what fraction of the bottle will be full?

   _____

Mathematics Practice

1. Which drawing shows $\frac{5}{8}$ of the figure shaded?

   Ⓐ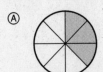

   Ⓑ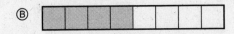

   Ⓒ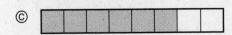

   Ⓓ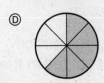

2. Which correctly compares the shaded parts of the figures?

   Ⓐ $\frac{1}{4} < \frac{1}{2}$

   Ⓑ $\frac{1}{4} > \frac{1}{2}$

   Ⓒ $\frac{1}{4} = \frac{1}{2}$

   Ⓓ $\frac{1}{2} < \frac{1}{4}$

3. Which of the following shows a fraction that is equivalent to $\frac{3}{4}$?

   Ⓐ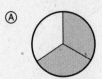

   Ⓑ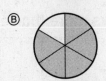

   Ⓒ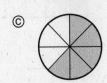

   Ⓓ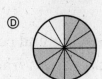

4. Felicia correctly answered $\frac{7}{10}$ of the questions on a test. What fraction of the test questions did Felicia **not** correctly answer?

Ⓐ $\frac{3}{10}$

Ⓑ $\frac{3}{7}$

Ⓒ $\frac{7}{3}$

Ⓓ $\frac{10}{3}$

5. Which figure shows more than $\frac{2}{3}$ shaded?

Ⓐ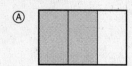

Ⓑ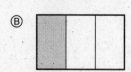

Ⓒ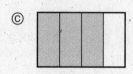

Ⓓ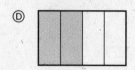

6. Which fraction correctly fills in the blank on the number line?

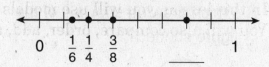

Ⓐ $\frac{4}{8}$

Ⓑ $\frac{5}{8}$

Ⓒ $\frac{6}{8}$

Ⓓ $\frac{7}{8}$

7. Which of the following correctly shows the fractions added in the model below?

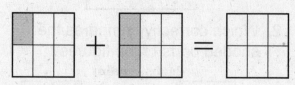

Ⓐ $\frac{1}{5} + \frac{2}{4} = \frac{3}{9}$

Ⓑ $\frac{1}{6} + \frac{2}{6} = \frac{3}{6}$

Ⓒ $\frac{1}{6} + \frac{2}{6} = \frac{3}{12}$

Ⓓ $\frac{1}{5} + \frac{2}{4} = \frac{7}{10}$

Lesson 4: Decimals

In this lesson, you will use models and place value to learn about decimals. You will also compare, order, add, and subtract decimals.

Decimals

A **decimal** is a number that shows tenths, hundredths, and so on by using a **decimal point**. Tenths represent a whole divided into 10 equal parts. Hundredths represent a whole divided into 100 equal parts.

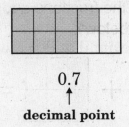

Example

In word form, 0.7 is written: **seven tenths**. The decimal 0.7 is represented by the shaded parts of the following figure.

0.7
↑
decimal point

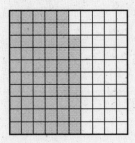

Example

In word form, 0.58 is written: **fifty-eight hundredths**. The decimal 0.58 is represented by the shaded parts of the following figure.

Place Value

Place-value tables show the value of each digit in a decimal.

Example

The following place-value table shows the decimals from the examples on page 49.

Ones	Decimal Point	Tenths	Hundredths
0	•	7	
0	•	5	8

Practice

Directions: For Numbers 1 through 4, write the decimal and the word form represented by the shaded parts of each figure.

1.

    decimal _____   word form _____

2.

    decimal _____   word form _____

3.

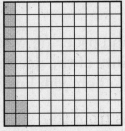

decimal _____   word form _____

4.

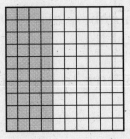

decimal _____   word form _____

Directions: For Numbers 5 through 7, write the digit that is in the given place value.

2.84

5. hundredths place _____

6. ones place _____

7. tenths place _____

Comparing and Ordering Decimals

Comparing and ordering decimals is a lot like comparing and ordering whole numbers. Just remember to always line up the decimal points of the decimals you will compare or order. You can use a place-value table to help you line up decimal points.

 Example

Compare 1.75 and 1.67.

Remember that the symbols you use to compare numbers are < (is less than), > (is greater than), and = (is equal to).

Step 1: **Write the decimals in a place-value table. Be sure to line up the decimal points.**

Ones	Decimal Point	Tenths	Hundredths
1	•	7	5
1	•	6	7

Step 2: **Start from the left column and compare the digits until they are different.**

Are the numbers in the ones column the same or different?

They are the same, so look at the numbers in the tenths column.

Are the numbers in the tenths column the same or different?

They are different. Which number has more tenths?

7 > 6

Therefore, 1.75 has more tenths than 1.67.

Step 3: **Compare the decimals using the correct symbol.**

1.75 > 1.67   or   1.67 < 1.75

Sometimes the decimals you compare will not have the same number of digits after the decimal point. When this happens, you must use zeros as placeholders.

Example

Compare 0.4 and 0.38.

Write the decimals in a place-value table. Be sure to line up the decimal points. Add a zero as a placeholder in the decimal 0.4.

Ones	Decimal Point	Tenths	Hundredths
0	•	4	0
0	•	3	8

When you order a set of decimals, you write the decimals from **least to greatest** or from **greatest to least**.

Example

Write these decimals in order from **greatest** to **least**.

0.51   0.54   0.49   0.5

Compare all the decimals so you are sure to write the largest decimal first and the smallest decimal last.

0.54   0.51   0.5   0.49

 TIP: Sometimes when you are ordering decimals, you will need to add zeros as placeholders in one or more of the decimals.

Practice

Directions: For Numbers 1 through 8, write the correct symbol ($<$, $>$, or $=$) to compare the decimals.

1. 0.25 _____ 0.52

2. 1.3 _____ 1.3

3. 0.8 _____ 0.9

4. 7.43 _____ 7.38

5. 0.67 _____ 0.7

6. 1.01 _____ 0.95

7. 0.39 _____ 0.32

8. 0.2 _____ 0.1

Directions: Use the following place-value table to help you answer Numbers 9 and 10.

Ones	Decimal Point	Tenths	Hundredths
0	•	8	3
	•		
	•		
	•		

9. Write the following decimals in the place-value table.

    0.95   1.03   0.8

10. Write the following decimals in order from **greatest** to **least**.

    0.83   0.95   1.03   0.8

Adding and Subtracting Decimals

You can use models to add decimals just like you used models to add fractions.

Example

Add: 0.23 + 0.45

Combine the shaded parts of both grids into one grid.

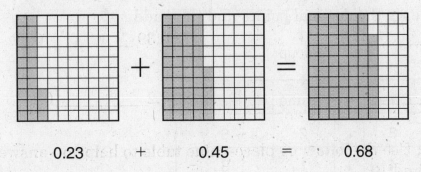

0.23   +   0.45   =   0.68

Therefore, 0.23 + 0.45 = 0.68.

Example

Subtract: 0.8 − 0.2

Cross out the shaded parts of the second rectangle from the first rectangle.

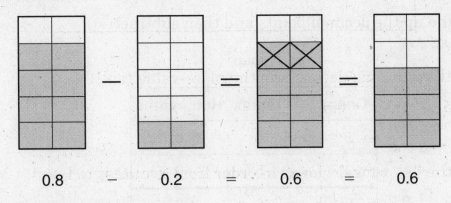

0.8   −   0.2   =   0.6   =   0.6

Therefore, 0.8 − 0.2 = 0.6.

You can also add and subtract decimals without models. When you use paper and pencil to add or subtract decimals, line up the place values and the decimal points. Then add or subtract like you would with whole numbers, but move the decimal point straight down into the sum. Don't forget to regroup and borrow, if necessary.

 Example

Add: 3.29 + 4.13

Line up the decimal points and then add.

regroup

Ones	•	Tenths	Hundredths
3	•	^{1}2	9
4	•	1	3
7	•	4	2

Therefore, 3.29 + 4.13 = 7.42.

Example

Subtract: 5.00 − 2.50

Line up the decimal points and then subtract.

regroup

	Ones	•	Tenths	Hundredths
borrow a one →	$\cancel{5}^{4}$	•	^{1}0	0
	2	•	5	0
	2	•	5	0

Therefore, 5.00 − 2.50 = 2.50.

Practice

Directions: For Numbers 1 and 2, write the decimal for the shaded parts of each figure. Then shade the sum or difference in the blank figure and write the decimal for the sum or difference.

1. 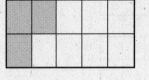 + 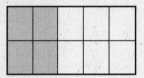 =

_____ + _____ = _____

2.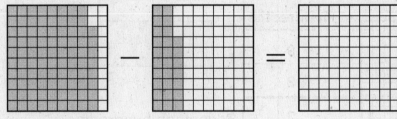

_____ − _____ = _____

Directions: For Numbers 3 through 8, line up the decimal points and then add or subtract.

3. $4.5 + 5.5 =$ _____

6. $6.25 + 17.75 =$ _____

4. $21.1 + 16.4 =$ _____

7. $12.99 - 6.44 =$ _____

5. $27.9 - 14.3 =$ _____

8. $143.50 - 31.61 =$ _____

Mathematics Practice

1. Which of the following correctly compares two decimals?

   Ⓐ 0.34 > 1.0

   Ⓑ 1.4 < 1.33

   Ⓒ 0.68 > 0.6

   Ⓓ 0.92 = 0.94

2. What decimal do the shaded parts of the following figure represent?

   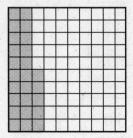

   Ⓐ 0.025

   Ⓑ 0.25

   Ⓒ 2.5

   Ⓓ 25

3. Add: 16.53 + 9.8

   Ⓐ 17.33

   Ⓑ 17.51

   Ⓒ 26.33

   Ⓓ 26.43

4. Which of the following shows three tenths shaded?

   Ⓐ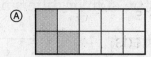

   Ⓑ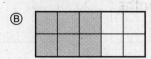

   Ⓒ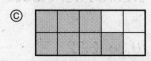

   Ⓓ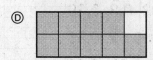

5. Seventeen hundredths of Annabel's rock collection is made up of white rocks. What decimal shows seventeen hundredths?

   Ⓐ 17.00

   Ⓑ 17.0

   Ⓒ 0.017

   Ⓓ 0.17

6. Subtract: 3.15 − 0.87

   Ⓐ 3.72

   Ⓑ 3.28

   Ⓒ 2.38

   Ⓓ 2.28

7. Chris read 0.2 of his book today. Which of these is the same as 0.2?

    Ⓐ two tenths

    Ⓑ two oneths

    Ⓒ two hundreds

    Ⓓ twenty tenths

8. Which list is ordered from **least** to **greatest**?

    Ⓐ 0.29, 0.3, 0.36, 0.32

    Ⓑ 0.36, 0.32, 0.3, 0.29

    Ⓒ 0.3, 0.29, 0.32, 0.36

    Ⓓ 0.29, 0.3, 0.32, 0.36

9. What decimal do the shaded parts of the following figure represent?

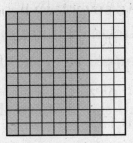

    Ⓐ 0.072

    Ⓑ 0.72

    Ⓒ 7.2

    Ⓓ 72

10. Subtract: $11.39 - 5.73$

    Ⓐ 5.36

    Ⓑ 5.66

    Ⓒ 6.36

    Ⓓ 7.66

11. Marla has a fish tank with 10 fish. Three of those fish are guppies. What decimal shows the fish in Marla's fish tank that are guppies?

    Ⓐ 0.7

    Ⓑ 0.6

    Ⓒ 0.3

    Ⓓ 0.1

12. Add: $5.8 + 3.4$

    Ⓐ 8.12

    Ⓑ 8.2

    Ⓒ 9.12

    Ⓓ 9.2

13. Which decimal has a 6 in the tenths place?

    Ⓐ 21.63

    Ⓑ 46.59

    Ⓒ 57.06

    Ⓓ 68.92

Lesson 5: Estimation and Problem Solving

In this lesson, you will review some useful ways to estimate answers. You will also review a strategy that can be used to solve problems.

Estimation

Estimation tells you what number the answer to a problem should be close to. You can use estimation before you find the exact answer to be sure your answer is **reasonable** (makes sense).

Rounding Whole Numbers

If you **round** the numbers from a problem to the nearest ten (10), hundred (100), or thousand (1,000), it will be easy for you to make a quick estimate of what the answer should be.

To round any whole number:

- **Circle** the digit in the place value **that is to be rounded**.

- **Underline** the digit in the place value **to the right** of the circled digit.

- The circled digit will either stay the same or increase by 1.

  If the underlined digit is **less than 5**, the circled digit **stays the same**.

  If the underlined digit is **greater than or equal to 5**, the circled digit **increases by 1**.

- Write **a zero or zeros** as placeholders for **all** the digits **to the right** of the circled digit.

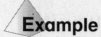 **Example**

Round 5,629 to the nearest hundred.

The 6 is in the hundreds place, so circle it. The 2 is to the right of the 6, so underline it.

$$5,\textcircled{6}\underline{2}9$$

Since 2 is less than 5, the 6 stays the same. Write zeros as placeholders in the tens and ones places.

5,629 rounded to the nearest hundred is 5,600.

You can use rounding to estimate the sum or difference of numbers when an exact answer is not necessary. Round each of the numbers to the nearest 10, 100, or 1,000, and then find the sum or difference of the rounded numbers. You will need to decide which place value you will round the numbers to before finding the sum or difference. Often, the place value you round to will depend on the numbers in the problem.

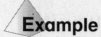 **Example**

Use rounding to estimate the following sum.

$$\begin{array}{r} 576 \\ + \ 349 \\ \hline \end{array}$$

In this example, round the numbers to the nearest hundred.

576 rounds to 600, and 349 rounds to 300.

Add the rounded numbers.

$$\begin{array}{r} 600 \\ + \ 300 \\ \hline 900 \end{array}$$

The estimated sum is 900. (The actual sum is 925.)

Practice

Directions: For Numbers 1 through 6, round each number to the given place value.

1. Round $6,427$ to the nearest ten. _____

2. Round $43,814$ to the nearest thousand. _____

3. Round 826 to the nearest hundred. _____

4. Round 385 to the nearest ten. _____

5. Round $7,106$ to the nearest hundred. _____

6. Round $92,497$ to the nearest thousand. _____

Directions: For Numbers 7 through 12, use rounding to estimate the sum or difference.

7.
$$\begin{array}{r} 94 \\ +\ 47 \\ \hline \end{array}$$

8.
$$\begin{array}{r} 843 \\ -\ 138 \\ \hline \end{array}$$

9.
$$\begin{array}{r} 61 \\ -\ 49 \\ \hline \end{array}$$

10.
$$\begin{array}{r} 8,587 \\ -\ 1,369 \\ \hline \end{array}$$

11.
$$\begin{array}{r} 82 \\ -\ 15 \\ \hline \end{array}$$

12.
$$\begin{array}{r} 5,187 \\ +\ 1,639 \\ \hline \end{array}$$

Rounding Decimals

Rounding decimals is similar to rounding whole numbers. To round a decimal to the nearest whole number, look at the number in the tenths place. If it is less than 5, the whole number stays the same. If it is 5 or greater, round up to the next whole number.

 Example

Round 2.82 to the nearest whole number.

The 8 is in the tenths place. Since 8 is greater than 5, round up.

Therefore, 2.82 rounded to the nearest whole number is 3.

You can also round decimals in computation problems. Round each decimal to the nearest whole number and then add or subtract.

Practice

Directions: For Numbers 1 through 4, round each decimal to the given place value.

1. Round 4.4 to the nearest whole number. _____

2. Round 8.5 to the nearest whole number. _____

3. Round 6.39 to the nearest whole number. _____

4. Round 5.62 to the nearest whole number. _____

Directions: For Numbers 5 and 6, use rounding to estimate the sum or difference.

5.   7.8
  + 4.6

6.   9.17
  − 3.70

Rounding Fractions

To round fractions, you must know if the given fraction is more or less than one half $\left(\frac{1}{2}\right)$. If it is less than $\frac{1}{2}$, the whole number stays the same. If it is $\frac{1}{2}$ or greater, round up to the next whole number.

 Example

Round $4\frac{2}{3}$ to the nearest whole number.

The fraction $\frac{2}{3}$ is greater than $\frac{1}{2}$, so round up to the next whole number.

Therefore, $4\frac{2}{3}$ rounded to the nearest whole number is 5.

You can also round fractions in computation problems. Round each fraction to the nearest whole number and then add or subtract.

Practice

Directions: For Numbers 1 through 4, round each fraction to the given place value.

1. Round $3\frac{1}{4}$ to the nearest whole number. _____

2. Round $6\frac{7}{8}$ to the nearest whole number. _____

3. Round $5\frac{3}{6}$ to the nearest whole number. _____

4. Round $9\frac{4}{10}$ to the nearest whole number. _____

Directions: For Numbers 5 and 6, use rounding to estimate the sum or difference.

5. $\quad 3\frac{1}{3}$
   $\quad + 2\frac{9}{10}$

6. $\quad 8\frac{3}{4}$
   $\quad - 4\frac{1}{2}$

Compatible Numbers

When you use compatible numbers to estimate, you change the numbers in the problem to make them easier to use. Then you can do the math easily in your head. The new numbers should be close to the original numbers. If you are adding more than two numbers, you can also change the order of the numbers to make it easier.

Example

Estimate the difference.

273 − 158

This problem would be difficult to do in your head because you need to borrow and regroup. Change 158 to 153 to make it easier.

273 − 153

Now you do not need to borrow and regroup: 2 hundreds take away 1 hundred is 1 hundred, 7 tens take away 5 tens is 2 tens, and 3 ones take away 3 ones is 0.

The difference is about 120. (The actual difference is 115.)

Example

Estimate the sum.

17 + 63 + 81 + 42

Switch 63 and 81 and then group the first two numbers and the last two numbers. The sum of each group is about 100.

(17 + 81) + (63 + 42)

100   +   100 = 200

The sum is about 200. (The actual sum is 203.)

Practice

Directions: For Numbers 1 through 8, use compatible numbers to estimate the sum or difference. Show your work in the space provided.

1. $132 + 364$

2. $82 - 54$

3. $556 - 148$

4. $355 + 549$

5. $706 + 93$

6. $945 - 398$

7. $38 + 93 + 59$

8. $73 + 48 + 54 + 32$

Mental Math

You can estimate the answer to computation problems, but there are times you need to find the exact answer. Most of the time you will use paper and pencil or a calculator to find the exact answer. However, there will be times that you can do the math in your head. This is called using **mental math**.

Example

Add: 31 + 28

Look at the problem. Since there are no numbers that need to be regrouped, this problem can be done in your head.

30 + 20 = 50 and 1 + 8 = 9

Therefore, 31 + 28 = 59.

Example

Subtract: 19,500 − 3,500

The numbers in this problem may be large, but they can be easily computed in your head.

19 − 3 = 16 and 500 − 500 = 000

Therefore, 19,500 − 3,500 = 16,000.

Practice

Directions: Use mental math to find the answers to Numbers 1 through 6.

1. 73 − 41 = _____

2. 110 + 70 = _____

3. 1,386 − 1,356 = _____

4. 57 + 32 = _____

5. 459 − 32 = _____

6. 361 + 33 = _____

Problem Solving

This step-by-step plan will help you solve word problems.

Step 1: **Understand the problem.** Decide what the problem is asking you to find. Write down the information that is given in the problem.

Step 2: **Make a plan.** Choose the correct operation (addition, subtraction, multiplication, or division) that is needed to solve the problem. Sometimes you will need to use more than one operation.

Step 3: **Estimate an answer.** Use rounding, front-end estimation, or regrouping to estimate an answer to be sure your actual answer is reasonable.

Step 4: **Solve the problem.** Do the math with the correct operation.

Step 5: **Check your answer.** Use the "opposite" operation to check. In Lesson 2, you saw that addition and subtraction are "opposites" and that multiplication and division are also "opposites."

Example

Use the step-by-step method to solve the following problem.

Phillip's dad bought 4 new T-shirts. He paid $9 for each T-shirt. How much did the T-shirts cost altogether?

Step 1: **Understand the problem.**

What is the problem asking you to find?

It is asking you to find the total cost of the 4 T-shirts.

What information is given in the problem?

Each T-shirt costs $9.

Step 2: **Make a plan.**

What is the correct operation needed to solve the problem?

To find the cost of all 4 T-shirts, given the cost of each T-shirt, you should use multiplication. (You can also use repeated addition.)

Step 3: **Estimate an answer.**

Use rounding to estimate an answer.

$$
\begin{array}{r}
10 \\
\times\ 4 \\
\hline
\end{array}
$$

The 4 T-shirts cost about $40 altogether.

Step 4: **Solve the problem.**

What is $9 multiplied by 4?

$$
\begin{array}{r}
9 \\
\times\ 4 \\
\hline
\end{array}
$$

The 4 T-shirts cost $36 altogether.

Step 5: **Check your answer.**

Division is the "opposite" of multiplication. To check a multiplication problem, use division.

$$
\begin{array}{r}
9 \\
4\overline{)36} \\
-\ 36 \\
\hline
0
\end{array}
$$

The answer of $36 is correct. (Notice that the correct answer is close to the estimate of $40.)

Practice

Directions: For Numbers 1 through 6, use the step-by-step method to solve each problem. Estimate the answer and find the actual answer.

1. Tamika has done 8 push-ups every morning for the last 7 days. How many total push-ups has Tamika done in the last 7 days?

   Tamika has done about _____ push-ups in the last 7 days.

   Tamika has done exactly_____ push-ups in the last 7 days.

2. Ticket sales for Saturday night's show totaled $345. Ticket sales for Sunday afternoon's show totaled $280. What were the total ticket sales for the two shows?

   The total ticket sales for the two shows were about _____.

   The total ticket sales for the two shows were exactly _____.

3. A total of 81 students have signed up for summer camp. They have been divided into 9 equal groups. How many students are in each group?

There are about _____ students in each group.

There are exactly _____ students in each group.

4. There are 8 boxes of cod fillets in the freezer. Each box contains 5 fillets. How many cod fillets are in the freezer?

There are about _____ cod fillets in the freezer.

There are exactly _____ cod fillets in the freezer.

5. Jeremy had $15.78 in his wallet. He spent $5.43 on lunch. How much money does Jeremy have left in his wallet?

Jeremy has about _____ left in his wallet.

Jeremy has exactly _____ left in his wallet.

6. Before dinner time, there were $3\frac{7}{8}$ pies at a restaurant. The restaurant served $2\frac{4}{8}$ pies to people for dessert. How many pies are left now?

There are about _____ pies left at the restaurant.

There are exactly _____ pies left at the restaurant.

People in Math

Euclid of Alexandria (about 325– 265 BCE)

Euclid lived about 2,400 years ago. He taught math and wrote many books. He is most famous for writing 13 books called *Elements of Geometry*. Students have studied Euclid's *Elements* for over 2,000 years. For this reason, Euclid may have been the most important math teacher of all time.

Why did Euclid's books last so long? Because they were very important to people. New copies of *Elements* were made over and over again. The books were also copied in many different languages.

After the Roman Empire fell, learning almost stopped. Many books on math and science were lost. But some Arabic countries were able to get copies of *Elements of Geometry*. Through trade with Arabic countries, Spain ended up with a copy of *Elements*. There it was translated into Latin.

Then, in 1450, the printing press was invented. For the first time, many people could get books. *Elements of Geometry* was first printed in 1482. It's been printed thousands of times since then. Now, you can even study it online!

Mathematics Practice

1. Which number sentence solves the following problem?

   Bob walked past 9 houses. Every house had 1 car parked in the driveway and 1 car parked in the street. How many parked cars did Bob see?

   Ⓐ $9 + 2 = 11$

   Ⓑ $9 \times 2 = 18$

   Ⓒ $9 - 2 = 7$

   Ⓓ $9 \times 1 \times 1 = 9$

2. Mrs. Mason's classroom has 28 desks. There are 4 desks in each row. How many rows of desks are there in Mrs. Mason's room?

   Ⓐ 7

   Ⓑ 8

   Ⓒ 24

   Ⓓ 32

3. Nick drove 621 miles on his vacation. Tom drove 254 miles on his vacation. Round to the nearest hundred to estimate how many miles Nick and Tom drove altogether.

   Ⓐ 600

   Ⓑ 700

   Ⓒ 800

   Ⓓ 900

4. In last night's basketball game, the Lions scored 67 points. Two nights ago, the Knights scored 82 points. How many more points did the Knights score than the Lions?

   Ⓐ 13

   Ⓑ 14

   Ⓒ 15

   Ⓓ 16

5. Brandy found a sale on shorts. She can buy 1 pair of shorts for $6. How much will 4 pairs of shorts cost?

   Ⓐ $20

   Ⓑ $24

   Ⓒ $28

   Ⓓ $30

6. Which is the **best** estimate of $68 - 19$?

   Ⓐ 60

   Ⓑ 55

   Ⓒ 50

   Ⓓ 45

7. The following table lists the numbers of students that attend three elementary schools.

Elementary School Students

Elementary School	Number of Students
Washington	375
Hamilton	422
Jefferson	297

Part A

Estimate the number of students at the three schools combined.

There are **about** _____ students at the three schools combined.

Part B

Find the actual number of students at the three schools combined.

There are _____ students at the three schools combined.

Part C

How close was your estimate to your actual answer? Is your answer reasonable?

_____

_____

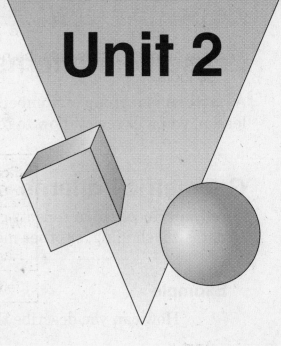

Unit 2

Algebra

What if every Monday morning when you get to school, your teacher gives you a math problem to do? What will you expect to happen when you get to school next Monday morning? You will most likely expect your teacher to give you a math problem to do. Why will you expect it? Because it's a pattern that has been happening over and over, every Monday morning.

In this unit, you will describe, extend, and study numerical and geometric patterns. You will use these patterns to solve problems. You will learn how to write expressions and number sentences. You will also learn how to solve open number sentences.

In This Unit

Patterns

Expressions and Number Sentences

Lesson 6: Patterns

A **pattern** is a group of numbers, shapes, or letters in a given order. In this lesson, you will review how to recognize, extend, and describe patterns.

Geometric Patterns

A **geometric pattern** repeats circles, squares, triangles, or any other shape. Order, size, shading, or other markings can also show a pattern.

Example

How can you describe this pattern?

There is 1 triangle, 1 square, 1 circle, 1 triangle, 1 square, and 1 circle.

What will the next figure in this pattern be?

The next figure will be a triangle.

Ways to Describe Shape Patterns

1. Look at the **shape** of the figures.
2. Look at the **size** of the figures.
3. Look at the **shading** or **markings** of the figures.

Practice

Directions: For Numbers 1 through 4, fill in the blanks to describe the shape pattern.

1. What are the shapes of the figures? Fill in the rest of the blanks.

  <u>circle</u>   <u>square</u>   _____   _____   _____   _____

2. What are the sizes of the figures? Fill in the rest of the blanks.

  <u>big</u>   <u>small</u>   _____   _____   _____   _____

3. What are the shapes of the figures? Fill in the blanks.

  _____   _____   _____   _____   _____   _____

4. What is the shading of the figures? Fill in the blanks.

  _____   _____   _____   _____   _____   _____

Addition and Subtraction Number Patterns

Number patterns are based on a rule. The rule tells you how to get from one number to the next number in the pattern. **Addition number patterns** are formed by adding from one number to the next. You add the same amount each time to reach the next number.

◢ **Example**

The road signs show an addition number pattern. What is the number of the last sign?

Highway 5	Highway 10	Highway 15	Highway 20	Highway

The rule for the pattern is add 5, or +5. The last sign is 25.

Subtraction number patterns are formed by subtracting from one number to the next. You subtract the same amount each time to reach the next number.

◢ **Example**

What is the rule for the pattern below?

24, 21, 18, 15, 12, 9, 6

Each number decreases by 3, so the rule is subtract 3, or −3.

Practice

Directions: For Numbers 1 through 5, write the next number in the pattern. Then write the rule for the pattern.

1. 15, 21, 27, 33, 39, 45, _____

   rule _____

2. 64, 59, 54, 49, 44, 39, _____

   rule _____

3. 72, 63, 54, 45, 36, 27, _____

   rule _____

4. 3, 12, 21, 30, 39, 48, _____

   rule _____

5. 22, 19, 16, 13, 10, 7, _____

   rule _____

6. What is the next number in the pattern?

   52, 45, 38, 31, 24, _____

   A. 16
   B. 17
   C. 18
   D. 19

Directions: For Numbers 7 through 14, fill in the missing number in the pattern.

7. 4, 11, 18, _____, 32, 39

8. 67, 65, 63, 61, _____, 57

9. 46, _____, 30, 22, 14, 6

10. 25, 27, 29, _____, 33, 35

11. 27, 23, 19, 15, _____, 7

12. 1, 6, 11, _____, 21, 26

13. 99, _____, 77, 66, 55, 44

14. 54, 48, 42, 36, _____, 24

15. What is the rule for the number pattern?

    8, 11, 14, 17, 20, 23

    A. add 3
    B. add 4
    C. subtract 3
    D. subtract 4

Multiplication and Division Number Patterns

In **multiplication number patterns**, the rule stays the same for the whole pattern. You multiply by the same amount each time to get to the next number.

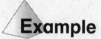 **Example**

Here is a multiplication number pattern. What is the rule for the pattern? What is the next number in the pattern?

3, 9, 27, 81, 243

Each number in the pattern is found by multiplying the number before it by 3. The rule is multiply by 3, or ×3.

243 × 3 = 729

The next number in the pattern is 729.

In **division number patterns**, the rule stays the same for the whole pattern. You divide by the same amount each time to get to the next number.

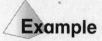 **Example**

Here is a division number pattern. What is the rule for the pattern? What is the next number in the pattern?

800, 400, 200, 100, 50

Each number in the pattern is found by dividing the number before it by 2. The rule is divide by 2, or ÷2.

50 ÷ 2 = 25

The next number in the pattern is 25.

Practice

Directions: For Numbers 1 through 5, write the next number in the pattern. Then write the rule for the pattern.

1. 4, 20, 100, _____

   rule _____

2. 80, 40, 20, 10, _____

   rule _____

3. 1, 4, 16, 64, _____

   rule _____

4. 81, 27, 9, _____

   rule _____

5. 2, 4, 8, 16, 32, 64, _____

   rule _____

6. What is the next number in the pattern?

   128, 32, 8, _____

   A. 6
   B. 4
   C. 2
   D. 0

Directions: For Numbers 7 through 14, fill in the missing number in the pattern.

7. 5, 25, _____, 625

8. 125, 25, _____, 1

9. 160, 80, _____, 20

10. 3, 6, 12, _____, 48

11. 2, 12, _____, 432

12. _____, 14, 28, 56

13. 216, 36, _____, 1

14. 2, 8, _____, 128

15. What is the rule for the number pattern?

   112, 56, 28, 14

   A. multiply by 2
   B. multiply by 3
   C. divide by 2
   D. divide by 3

Number Patterns in Tables

You can use patterns in tables to help you solve problems. A **table** shows how one value is related to another.

Function Tables

A **function table** matches each input value with an output value. You can find rules in function tables going from the input value to the output value.

 **Example**

Find the missing number in column B in the function table.

A		B
1	→	4
2	→	5
3	→	6
4	→	7
5	→	☐

The **input** values are in column A and the **output** values are in column B. You put *in* values into column A and get *out* values from column B. The rule going from column A to column B in the function table is add 3.

To find the missing value in the function table, use the rule. Add 3 to the input value of 5 in column A. The missing number in column B is 5 + 3, or 8.

You can also use a table to describe how a change in one value results in a change in a second value. For example, look at the table in the example above. Notice that each time the value of the number in column A increases by 1, the value of the number in column B also increases by 1. To find the missing number, you could just add 1 to 7 to get 8.

Practice

Directions: For Numbers 1 through 6, find the missing value in the function table.

1.

A		B
10	→	9
9	→	8
8	→	7
7	→	6
6	→	☐

4.

A		B
1	→	5
3	→	15
5	→	25
7	→	☐
9	→	45

2.

A		B
2	→	7
4	→	9
6	→	11
8	→	13
10	→	☐

5.

A		B
10	→	8
8	→	6
6	→	4
4	→	2
2	→	☐

3.

A		B
1	→	3
2	→	6
3	→	9
4	→	☐
5	→	15

6.

A		B
2	→	8
4	→	16
6	→	24
8	→	☐
10	→	40

Solving Problems

You can use patterns to help you solve problems.

◢ **Example**

> A baby alligator measured 8 inches long when it was born. If the baby alligator grows 12 inches every year, how long will it be when it is 3 years old?
>
> Start with the number 8. Add 12 a total of 3 times.
>
> $8 + 12 = 20$ (1 time)
>
> $20 + 12 = 32$ (2 times)
>
> $32 + 12 = 44$ (3 times)
>
> The baby alligator will be 44 inches long when it is 3 years old.
>
> You can also use a **table** to find the answer. Use the same pattern as before. Add 12 inches for each year for 3 years.

Age	At birth	1 year	2 years	3 years
Height	8 inches	20 inches	32 inches	44 inches

> From the table, you can see that the alligator will be 44 inches long when it is 3 years old.

Practice

Directions: Use the following information to answer Numbers 1 and 2.

John put 5 pennies into his piggy bank. Each day, he will put 1 more penny into the piggy bank than the day before. John's mom said she will put twice the number of pennies into John's piggy bank that he does.

Day	1	2	3	4	5	6	7
John	5	6	7	8	9	10	11
Mom	10	12	14	16	18	20	

1. How many pennies will John's mom put into his piggy bank on the seventh day?

   _____

2. What is the rule for the pattern going from John's number of pennies to his mom's number of pennies?

   A. add 2

   B. subtract 2

   C. multiply by 2

   D. divide by 2

3. Every stoplight in Danny's neighborhood near Fort Myers has 3 colored lights (1 red, 1 yellow, and 1 green). There are 7 stoplights in Danny's neighborhood. How many colored lights are there?

   _____

Stoplights	1	2	3	4	5	6	7
Colored Lights	3	6	9	12	15	18	

4. Third graders are blowing up balloons for the school carnival. If the pattern continues, how many balloons will the third graders have blown up by 1:00 P.M.?

_____

Time	Number of Balloons
9:00 A.M.	30
10:00 A.M.	55
11:00 A.M.	80
12:00 P.M.	105
1:00 P.M.	

5. An ant has 6 legs. How many legs do 6 ants have? _____

Ants	1	2	3	4	5	6
Legs	6	12	18	24	30	

6. A horse has 4 legs. There are 5 horses on Jo's farm. Which table correctly shows the number of legs the 5 horses on Jo's farm have?

A.

Horses	1	2	3	4	5
Legs	4	8	10	12	16

B.

Horses	1	2	3	4	5
Legs	4	8	12	15	18

C.

Horses	1	2	3	4	5
Legs	4	8	12	16	20

D.

Horses	1	2	3	4	5
Legs	4	7	11	15	19

Mathematics Practice

1. What is the next number in the following multiplication number pattern?

    1, 2, 4, _____

    Ⓐ   6
    Ⓑ   8
    Ⓒ 12
    Ⓓ 16

2. Which figure is missing from the shape pattern?

    Ⓐ ▢
    Ⓑ ▢
    Ⓒ ◯
    Ⓓ ◯

3. Which pattern has a rule of add 13?

    Ⓐ 9, 24, 39, 54, 69, 84
    Ⓑ 1, 13, 25, 37, 49, 61
    Ⓒ 7, 21, 35, 49, 63, 77
    Ⓓ 8, 21, 34, 47, 60, 73

4. What is the missing number in the following function table?

A	B
1 →	2
2 →	4
3 →	6
4 →	▢
5 →	10

    Ⓐ   8
    Ⓑ   9
    Ⓒ 10
    Ⓓ 12

5. What is the missing number in the following subtraction number pattern?

   40, 32, _____, 16, 8, 0

   Ⓐ 24
   Ⓑ 23
   Ⓒ 22
   Ⓓ 21

6. Each student in Mrs. Bendlin's class earns 35 points for every 5 books he or she reads.

Books Read	Points Earned
5	35
10	70
15	105
20	140
25	

   Lesley has read 25 books. How many points has Lesley earned?

   Ⓐ 165
   Ⓑ 170
   Ⓒ 175
   Ⓓ 180

7. What is the next number in the following division number pattern?

   135, 45, 15, _____

   Ⓐ 3
   Ⓑ 5
   Ⓒ 15
   Ⓓ 30

8. An octopus has 8 arms. Which table correctly shows the number of arms for the number of octopuses?

   Ⓐ
Octopuses	2	3	4	5
Arms	14	22	30	38

   Ⓑ
Octopuses	2	3	4	5
Arms	15	23	31	39

   Ⓒ
Octopuses	2	3	4	5
Arms	16	24	32	40

   Ⓓ
Octopuses	2	3	4	5
Arms	17	25	33	41

Lesson 7: Expressions and Number Sentences

Algebra is the study of the relationships between numbers. Some of the numbers are known, but others are missing. Often, you must find the values of the missing numbers in a relationship. The missing numbers may be shown by a $\bigcirc$, $\square$, $\triangle$, $\triangledown$, _____, or any other symbol. Missing numbers may also be shown by letters called **variables**. For example, a, b, c, n, x, y, or z may stand for missing numbers.

Expressions

Expressions are numbers by themselves or numbers written using an operation symbol ($+$, $-$, $\times$, or $\div$). The **value** of an expression is the number the expression shows.

Example

Here are some examples of expressions and their values.

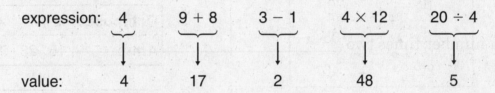

expression:	4	9 + 8	3 − 1	4 × 12	20 ÷ 4
value:	4	17	2	48	5

Expressions can also be written if there is a number missing.

Examples

"Six more than a number" can be written as $\square + 6$.

"A number times seven" can be written as $n \times 7$.

"Eight less than a number" can be written as $\triangledown - 8$.

"Twenty-eight divided by a number" can be written as $28 \div b$.

Practice

Directions: For Numbers 1 through 8, write the expression using a number, a variable or symbol, and a sign (+, −, ×, or ÷).

1. two fewer than a number _____

2. ten divided by a number _____

3. six times a number _____

4. seven more than a number _____

5. a number divided by five _____

6. sixteen minus a number _____

7. a number times two _____

8. thirteen plus a number _____

Directions: For Numbers 9 through 12, write the expression in words.

9. $\bigcirc + 12$ _____

10. $4 \times n$ _____

11. $14 - c$ _____

12. $\square \div 2$ _____

Number Sentences

Number sentences (also called **equations**) are two expressions of the same value that are joined by an **equals sign (=)**. Two expressions that are **not** the same value can be joined by a **not equals sign (≠)**.

 Example

Here are some examples of number sentences.

$$3 + 4 = 7 \qquad 8 \times 2 = 16 \qquad 24 \div 2 = 12 \qquad 18 = 24 - 6$$

$$7 \quad = 7 \qquad 16 \quad = 16 \qquad 12 \quad = 12 \qquad 18 = \quad 18$$

Open Number Sentences

In an **open number sentence**, one or more of the numbers from one or both expressions may be missing.

 Example

Here are some examples of open number sentences:

$$\bigcirc + 5 = 9$$

$$8 \times n = 40$$

$$\square - \triangledown = 12$$

$$18 \div 6 = x$$

Solving Open Number Sentences

You can use addition, subtraction, multiplication, or division facts to find the missing number in an open number sentence.

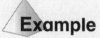**Example**

What number belongs in place of the $\triangledown$ in this open number sentence?

$$8 + \triangledown = 14$$

You must find out what number added to 8 will equal 14. Find the number that belongs to the addition and subtraction fact family 8, $\triangledown$, 14. To do so, use subtraction to make another number sentence in the fact family.

$$14 - 8 = \mathbf{6}$$

The number 6 belongs in place of the $\triangledown$. (You can say that $\triangledown = 6$.)

Example

What number belongs in place of the $\square$ in this open number sentence?

$$\square \div 5 = 2$$

You must find out what number divided by 5 equals 2. Find the number that belongs to the multiplication and division fact family $\square$, 5, 2. To do so, use multiplication to make another number sentence in the fact family.

$$2 \times 5 = \mathbf{10}$$

The number 10 belongs in place of the $\square$. (You can say that $\square = 10$.)

Practice

Directions: For Numbers 1 through 10, find the number that belongs in place of the symbol or variable in each open number sentence.

1. $3 + y = 7$

$y = $ _____

2. $\square - 9 = 13$

$\square = $ _____

3. $18 - \triangle = 6$

$\triangle = $ _____

4. $7 + z = 16$

$z = $ _____

5. $\bigcirc + 8 = 9$

$\bigcirc = $ _____

6. $2 \times y = 12$

$y = $ _____

7. $9 \div \bigcirc = 3$

$\bigcirc = $ _____

8. $14 \div b = 7$

$b = $ _____

9. $8 \times \triangle = 16$

$\triangle = $ _____

10. $5 \times z = 5$

$z = $ _____

11. What number belongs in place of the _____ in the following open number sentence?

$$12 - \underline{\quad} = 5$$

A. 4
B. 5
C. 6
D. 7

12. What number belongs in place of the r in the following open number sentence?

$$18 \div r = 6$$

A. 2
B. 3
C. 4
D. 5

Solving Word Problems

You can solve word problems by writing an open number sentence that shows the information from the problem. The symbol or variable will stand for the value of the missing number.

◢ **Example**

Josie has a bag of marbles. She gave 11 of the marbles to her friend Gloria. She now has 7 left. How many marbles did Josie start with?

The following open number sentence shows the information from the problem.

number of marbles → $n - 11 = 7$ ← **number of marbles left**
she started with
(the missing number)   **number of marbles she gave away**

What number belongs in place of the n in the open number sentence?

$n - 11 = 7$

$18 - 11 = 7$ (Since 7 + 11 = 18, 18 − 11 = 7.)

Josie started with 18 marbles.

◢ **Example**

Davy's favorite ride at the amusement park has 4 cars. A total of 20 people can ride in the 4 cars altogether. How many people can ride in each car?

The following open number sentence shows the information from the problem.

number of cars → $4 \times \triangledown = 20$ ← **total number of people who**
on the ride   **can ride in the 4 cars altogether**
number of people that can ride in each car
(the missing number)

What number belongs in place of the $\triangledown$ in the open number sentence?

$4 \times \triangledown = 20$

$4 \times 5 = 20$ (Since 20 ÷ 4 = 5, 4 × 5 = 20)

Five people can ride in each car.

Practice

Directions: For Numbers 1 through 6, write an open number sentence that shows the information from the problem. Write what each number, symbol, or variable stands for. Then solve the open number sentence.

1. Missy has 7 goldfish in her fish tank. She has a total of 15 fish in her fish tank. How many of the fish in Missy's fish tank are **not** goldfish?

2. Pablo has gone running for 10 days in a row. He ran the same number of miles each day. He ran 20 miles in all. How many miles did Pablo run each day?

3. There are 18 students in Mrs. White's class. Some students are absent today. There are 15 students in class right now. How many students are absent?

4. Rob has 30 toy cars. He put them in equal-sized groups. There are 6 cars in each group. How many groups of cars does Rob have?

5. Jade has a bag of apples. He gave 3 apples to his sister. Now there are 12 apples in the bag. How many apples did Jade start with?

6. Last year, Shania's dog weighed 13 pounds. Now he weighs 18 pounds. How many pounds has Shania's dog gained in the last year?

Mathematics Practice

1. What number belongs in place of the ▽ in this open number sentence?

$$10 - \triangledown = 8$$

Ⓐ 0
Ⓑ 2
Ⓒ 8
Ⓓ 18

2. What number belongs in place of the *n* in this open number sentence?

$$9 + 3 = n$$

Ⓐ 3
Ⓑ 6
Ⓒ 9
Ⓓ 12

3. Tanya has 3 sisters. She also has some brothers. Altogether, Tanya has 8 sisters and brothers. Which open number sentence shows how to find out how many brothers Tanya has?

Ⓐ $3 + b = 8$
Ⓑ $3 + 8 = b$
Ⓒ $b - 3 = 8$
Ⓓ $b - 8 = 3$

4. What number belongs in place of the *y* in this open number sentence?

$$4 \times y = 16$$

Ⓐ 2
Ⓑ 4
Ⓒ 8
Ⓓ 12

5. What number belongs in place of the ☐ in this open number sentence?

$$20 \div \square = 2$$

Ⓐ 2
Ⓑ 5
Ⓒ 10
Ⓓ 18

6. Which means the same as "four less than a number"?

Ⓐ $4 - \square$
Ⓑ $4 + \square$
Ⓒ $\square - 4$
Ⓓ $\square + 4$

7. Which situation matches this open number sentence?

$$14 - \triangle = 10$$

Ⓐ Donald had 14 marbles. He gave some away. He then had 10 left. How many marbles did Donald give away?

Ⓑ Marie had 10 marbles. She found 14 more. How many marbles did Marie have?

Ⓒ Gena had some marbles. She bought 10 more. Then she had 14. How many marbles did Gena start with?

Ⓓ Gary had some marbles. He gave 10 away. Then he had 14. How many marbles did Gary start with?

8. Tina has 18 orange slices. She divides them equally among the players on her basketball team. Each player gets 2 orange slices. How many players are on Tina's basketball team?

Part A
Write an open number sentence that shows the information from the problem. Write what each number, symbol, or variable stands for.

Part B
Solve the open number sentence.

There are _____ players on Tina's basketball team.

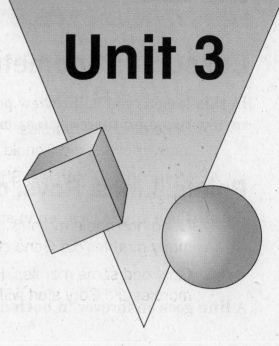

Unit 3

Geometry

There are all kinds of geometric figures in the objects around you. Once you start looking, you will see triangles, circles, rectangles, cubes, cones, spheres, and other figures in all kinds of things.

In this unit, you will describe two- and three-dimensional figures. You will draw and classify two-dimensional figures according to their number of sides. You will identify, locate, and plot points on grids. You will explore symmetry. You will also recognize congruent and similar figures, slides, flips, and turns.

In This Unit

Geometric Figures

Geometric Concepts

Lesson 8: Geometric Figures

In this lesson, you will review points, lines, rays, and angles. You will also review two- and three-dimensional figures.

Points, Lines, Rays, and Angles

A **point** is a single location in space.

●

A **line** goes on forever in **both** directions.

When two lines meet, they are called **intersecting lines**.

Lines that meet and form right angles are called **perpendicular lines**.

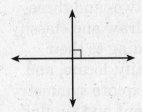

Lines that never meet are called **parallel lines**.

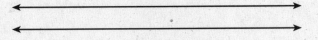

A **ray** is a part of a line that goes on forever in **one** direction.

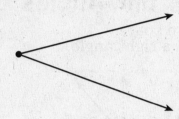

An **angle** is made up of two rays that share the same endpoint. The shared endpoint is called the **vertex**.

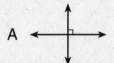

Practice

Directions: For Numbers 1 through 5, write the letter of the drawing in the blank next to the correct name.

1. line _____

2. ray _____

3. perpendicular lines _____

4. parallel lines _____

5. intersecting lines _____

A

B

C

D

E

6. Circle the picture that contains parallel lines.

Kinds of Angles

A **right angle** looks like a square corner.

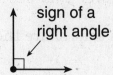

sign of a
right angle

An **acute** angle is **less than** a right angle.

less than a
right angle

An **obtuse** angle is **greater than** a right angle.

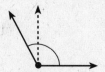

greater than a
right angle

A **straight angle** looks like a line. It is made of two rays pointing in opposite directions.

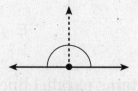

a **straight** angle
or line

Practice

1. Match each angle with the words that describe it. The first one has been done for you.

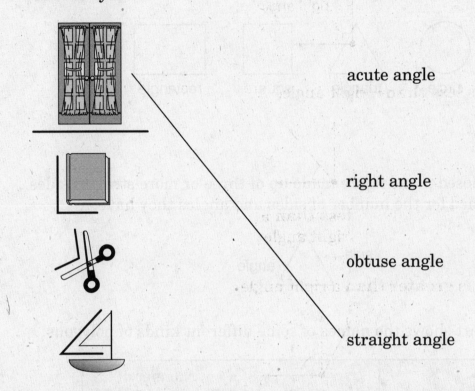

acute angle

right angle

obtuse angle

straight angle

Directions: For Numbers 2 through 5, use a straightedge to draw an example of the given kind of angle.

2. obtuse angle

4. right angle

3. straight angle

5. acute angle

Two-Dimensional Figures

Two-dimensional (flat) **figures** such as circles, triangles, squares, and rectangles are called plane figures. They lie on a flat surface. The following are some examples of plane figures.

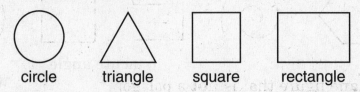

circle   triangle   square   rectangle

Polygons

A **polygon** is a closed plane figure made up of three or more straight sides. Polygons are named for the number of sides and angles they have.

side →

angle

The following chart shows the names of some different kinds of polygons.

Polygon	Name	Number of Sides and Angles
△	triangle	3
▭	quadrilateral	4
⬠	pentagon	5
⬡	hexagon	6
⯃	octagon	8

➡ **TIP: Squares** and **rectangles** are kinds of quadrilaterals.

104

Practice

1. Color the plane figures that are polygons.

2. Color the plane figure that is **not** a polygon.

What is the name of the plane figure you colored? _____

Why is the figure you colored **not** a polygon? _____

_____

3. Draw a line from each real-life object to the polygon it reminds you of.

triangle   pentagon   hexagon   quadrilateral   octagon

Directions: For Numbers 4 through 6, write the name of the polygon with the given number of sides and angles.

4. 5 sides and 5 angles _____

5. 3 sides and 3 angles _____

6. 8 sides and 8 angles _____

Directions: For Numbers 7 and 8, draw an example of the given polygon in the space provided.

7. hexagon

8. quadrilateral

9. Which of the following polygons is **not** a triangle?

   A.

   B.

   C.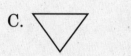

   D.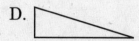

10. Which of the following polygons is a quadrilateral?

   A.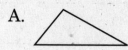

   B.

   C.

   D.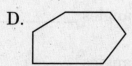

11. Look at the following plane figures. In the spaces provided, write one way in which the figures are alike and one way in which they are different.

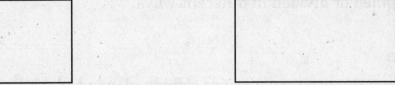

alike _____

_____

different _____

_____

12. Look at the following plane figures. In the spaces provided, write one way in which the figures are alike and one way in which they are different.

 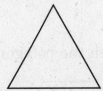

alike _____

_____

different _____

_____

Combining and Dividing Polygons

You can combine and divide polygons to make different polygons. Polygons can be combined or divided in different ways.

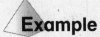 **Example**

When the two triangles are combined, what plane figure is made?

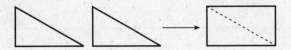

The two triangles make a rectangle.

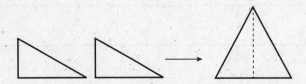

The two triangles can also be combined to make a bigger triangle.

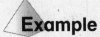 **Example**

When the polygon is cut in half, what two plane figures are made?

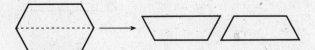

The polygon makes two quadrilaterals.

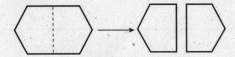

The polygon can also be divided to make two pentagons.

Practice

Directions: For Numbers 1 through 4, draw the polygon given by using the figures shown.

1. pentagon

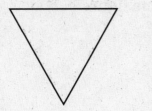

2. rectangle

3. square

4. triangle

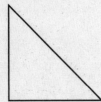

Directions: For Numbers 5 through 8, draw lines on each figure to form the given polygons.

5. 3 triangles

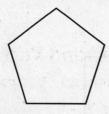

6. 2 pentagons

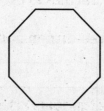

7. 1 triangle and 1 quadrilateral

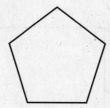

8. 2 triangles and 2 quadrilaterals

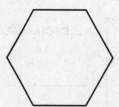

Three-Dimensional Figures

Three-dimensional (not flat) **figures** are sometimes called solid figures. They have length, width, and height. Some three-dimensional figures have faces, edges, and vertices. Other three-dimensional figures have curves.

Figures with Faces, Edges, and Vertices

The figure below defines face, edge, and vertex.

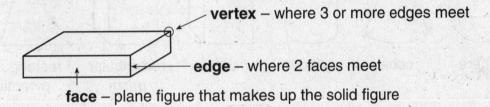

vertex – where 3 or more edges meet

edge – where 2 faces meet

face – plane figure that makes up the solid figure

The following table shows the three-dimensional figures that have faces, edges, and vertices.

Cube	Rectangular Prism	Rectangular Pyramid
6 faces 12 edges 8 vertices	6 faces 12 edges 8 vertices	5 faces 8 edges 5 vertices

Figures with Curves

The following table shows the three-dimensional figures that have curves.

Sphere	Cylinder	Cone
Does not have faces, edges, or vertices.	2 circular faces	1 circular face

Practice

Directions: For Numbers 1 through 3, read the sentence. Then write the letter of each three-dimensional figure that is described by the sentence. You may have more than one answer for each.

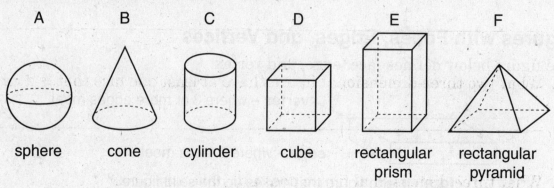

A   B   C   D   E   F

sphere   cone   cylinder   cube   rectangular prism   rectangular pyramid

1. They have a curved surface. _____

2. They have more edges than faces. _____

3. They have the same number of vertices as edges. _____

4. Under each object, write the name of the three-dimensional figure it reminds you of.

_____   _____   _____

_____   _____   _____

Objectives: G.A.3, G.A.4

Directions: Use the names of the three-dimensional figures on page 111 to answer Numbers 5 through 9.

5. What two three-dimensional figures have the same numbers of faces, vertices, and edges as each other?

_____

6. What two three-dimensional figures have at least one face that is a circle?

_____

7. What three-dimensional figure does **not** have any faces?

_____

8. What three-dimensional figure has four faces that are triangles?

_____

9. What three-dimensional figure has an odd number of vertices?

_____

10. Shade the following three-dimensional figures that are made up of all flat faces.

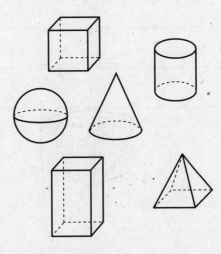

11. Look at the following three-dimensional figures. In the spaces provided, write one way in which the figures are alike and one way in which they are different.

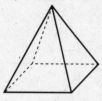 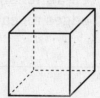

alike _____

_____

different _____

_____

12. Look at the following three-dimensional figures. In the spaces provided, write one way in which the figures are alike and one way in which they are different.

alike _____

_____

different _____

_____

Mathematics Practice

1. What figure has only 3 angles?

   Ⓐ circle

   Ⓑ triangle

   Ⓒ square

   Ⓓ rectangle

2. Which figure is a pentagon?

   Ⓐ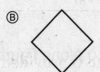

   Ⓑ

   Ⓒ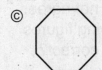

   Ⓓ

3. Which triangle has a right angle?

   Ⓐ

   Ⓑ

   Ⓒ

   Ⓓ

4. Which object looks like a cube the most?

   Ⓐ

   Ⓑ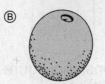

   Ⓒ

   Ⓓ

5. What plane figure has no straight sides and no angles?

Ⓐ hexagon

Ⓑ square

Ⓒ triangle

Ⓓ circle

6. What plane figure are the faces of a cylinder?

Ⓐ

Ⓑ

Ⓒ

Ⓓ

7. Which three-dimensional figure has exactly 1 face?

Ⓐ sphere

Ⓑ cone

Ⓒ cylinder

Ⓓ cube

8. Which is one way these figures are alike?

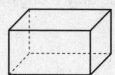

Ⓐ They both have curved surfaces.

Ⓑ They both have 4 faces that are triangles.

Ⓒ They both have the same number of faces.

Ⓓ They both have at least 1 rectangular face.

9. Ashley says that if a plane figure has four sides, it must be a square. Josh does not agree. Which of the following figures shows that Josh is correct?

Ⓐ

Ⓑ

Ⓒ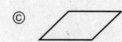

Ⓓ

10. Which three-dimensional figure has exactly 5 vertices?

Ⓐ

Ⓑ

Ⓒ

Ⓓ

11. Which polygon has four right angles?

Ⓐ octagon

Ⓑ rectangle

Ⓒ trapezoid

Ⓓ triangle

12. Which of these shows perpendicular lines?

Ⓐ

Ⓑ

Ⓒ

Ⓓ

13. Which of these three-dimensional figures is a sphere?

Ⓐ

Ⓑ

Ⓒ

Ⓓ

Lesson 9: Geometric Concepts

In this lesson, you will use grids to solve problems. You will explore symmetry, similar and congruent figures, and transformations.

Grids

A **grid** is used to locate objects or places. A set of two numbers, such as (2, 8), gives the object's location. This pair is an **ordered pair**. The first number tells you how far to go across. The second number tells you how far to go up.

Example

Look at the following grid. Where is Walnut Grove located?

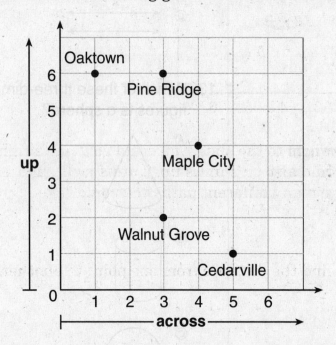

To get to Walnut Grove, you go across to 3. Then you go up to 2. Walnut Grove is located at (3, 2).

Grids can also be used to describe paths from one point to another.

 Example

Look at the following grid. Describe a path between the swings and the slide.

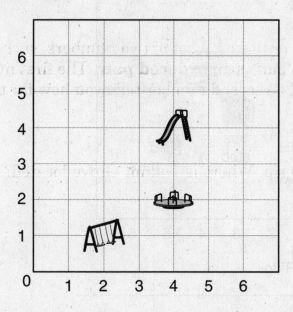

To get from the swings to the slide, you could go 2 units right and 3 units up. You could also go 2 units up, 2 units right, and 1 more unit up. There are many different paths you could take.

Grids can also be used to find the distance from one point to another.

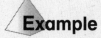 **Example**

Look at the grid in the example above. What is the distance between the slide and the merry-go-round?

Count the number of units between the slide and the merry-go-round. The distance between them is 2 units.

Practice

Directions: Use the grid below to answer Numbers 1 through 6.

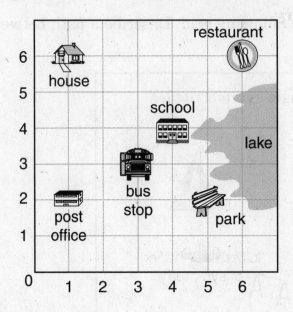

1. What is located at (1, 6)? _____

2. Where is the restaurant located? _____

3. The grocery store is located at (0, 4). Plot and label a point to show where the grocery store is located.

4. Where is the bus stop located? _____

5. Describe a path between the house and the school.

    _____

6. What is the distance between the park and the post office?

    _____

Symmetry

A plane figure has **symmetry** when it can be folded in half so that one half fits exactly onto the other. The line across which the plane figure is folded is the **line of symmetry**.

 Example

How many lines of symmetry does this star have?

Is this triangle symmetrical?

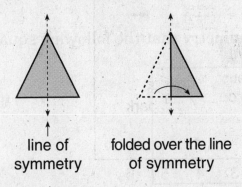

line of   folded over the line
symmetry   of symmetry

Yes, the triangle is symmetrical because it can be folded over a line of symmetry.

Some plane figures have more than one line of symmetry.

 Example

How many lines of symmetry does this star have?

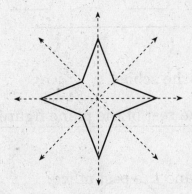

This four-pointed star could be folded in half 4 different ways, so the star has 4 lines of symmetry.

Practice

1. Draw a circle around each of the following letters that does **not** have a line of symmetry.

Q W V O U P

2. Draw all the different lines of symmetry that the following square has.

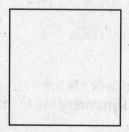

How many lines of symmetry does the square have? _____

Directions: For Numbers 3 and 4, circle the figure that shows a line of symmetry.

3.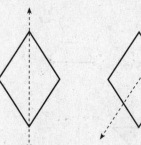

4.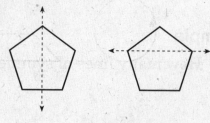

Directions: For Numbers 5 and 6, draw the rest of the plane figure, given half of the figure and the line of symmetry.

5.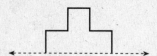

6.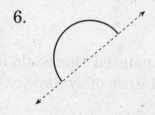

Similar Figures

Plane figures that have the same shape are **similar figures**. Similar figures can be the same size or different sizes.

 Example

Each pair of figures below is similar.

Practice

1. Circle each pair of plane figures that is similar.

2. Draw a line to connect each pair of similar figures.

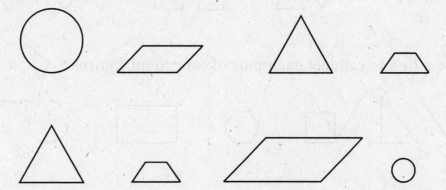

Congruent Figures

Plane figures that have the same shape and the same size are **congruent figures**. Congruent figures are an exact match.

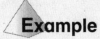 **Example**

Look at the pairs of plane figures.

The squares on the left are the same shape but not the same size. They are not congruent. The squares on the right are the same shape and size. They are congruent.

Practice

1. Circle each pair of plane figures that is congruent.

2. Draw a line to connect each pair of congruent figures.

Transformations

A **transformation** happens when you move a figure by sliding, flipping, or turning it. Sliding, flipping, or turning a figure will not change the size or the shape of the figure.

Slide

When you slide a figure in one direction, the movement is a **translation**. The figure can be slid in any direction.

Flip

When you flip a figure over a line, the movement is a **reflection**. Think of a flip as what the figure would look like in the mirror.

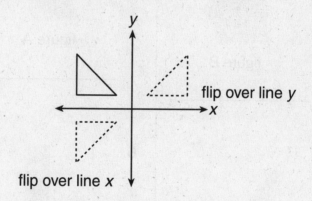

flip over line *y*

flip over line *x*

Turn

When you turn a figure around a point, the movement is a **rotation**. Figures may be turned in either a clockwise or counterclockwise direction.

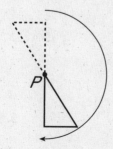

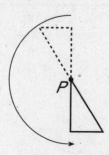

180° clockwise turn   180° counterclockwise turn

Practice

Directions: For Numbers 1 through 6, write whether a *slide*, *flip*, or *turn* was used to go from figure A to figure B.

1.

figure A   figure B

_____

4.

figure A   figure B

_____

2.

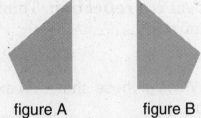

figure A   figure B

_____

5.

figure A   figure B

_____

3.

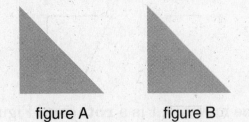

figure A   figure B

_____

6.

figure A   figure B

_____

Mathematics Practice

1. Which two figures are similar?

Ⓐ

Ⓑ

Ⓒ

Ⓓ

2. Which of these shows an example of a slide?

Ⓐ

Ⓑ

Ⓒ

Ⓓ

3. Which shows the correct line of symmetry on the figure?

Ⓐ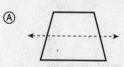

Ⓑ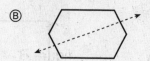

Ⓒ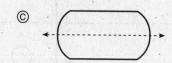

Ⓓ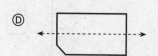

4. Which of these shows an example of a flip?

Ⓐ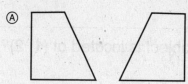

Ⓑ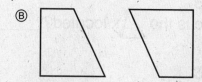

Ⓒ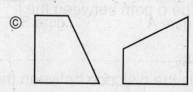

Ⓓ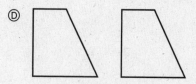

5. Which two figures are congruent?

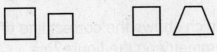

Ⓐ   Ⓑ   Ⓒ   Ⓓ

6. Look at the following grid.

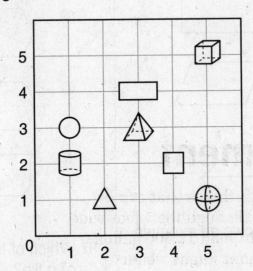

Part A
What object is located at (1, 2)? _____

Part B
Where is the 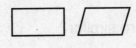 located? _____

Part C
Describe a path between the ▭ and the △: _____

Part D
What is the distance between the 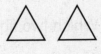 and the ⊕? _____

Unit 4

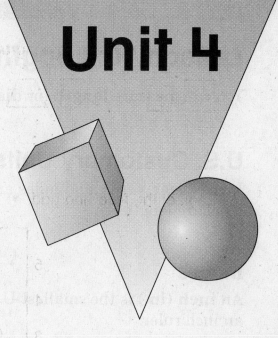

Measurement

The world is filled with things that can be measured. A rain puddle might be 1 foot wide, a swimming pool might hold 12,500 gallons of water, and an elephant might weigh 5,000 kilograms.

In this unit, you will measure the length, weight, and capacity of objects. You will tell time using both analog and digital clocks. You will measure temperature in both degrees Fahrenheit and degrees Celsius. You will find the perimeter and area of two-dimensional figures. You will also find the volume of rectangular prisms.

In This Unit

Length

Weight

Capacity

Time and Temperature

Geometric Measurement

Lesson 10: Length

You can measure **length** (or **distance**) using U.S. customary or metric units.

U.S. Customary Units of Length

Inches, feet, yards, and miles are some of the U.S. customary units used to measure length.

Inches

An **inch (in.)** is the smallest U.S. customary unit. To measure in inches, use an inch ruler.

▷ Example

The distance from the tip of your thumb to the first knuckle is about an inch.

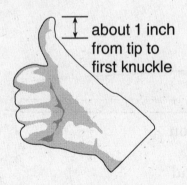

▷ Example

What is the length of the following pencil to the nearest half inch?

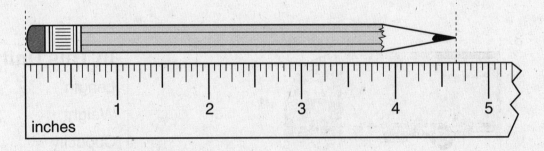

The pencil is about $4\frac{1}{2}$ inches long.

Practice

Directions: For Numbers 1 through 3, estimate the length of each object to the nearest inch. Then measure each object with an inch ruler to the nearest half inch.

1.

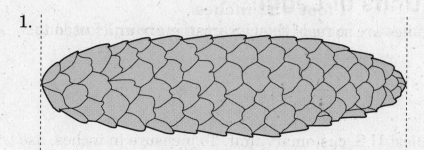

Estimate: about _____ in.   **Measurement:** _____ in.

2.

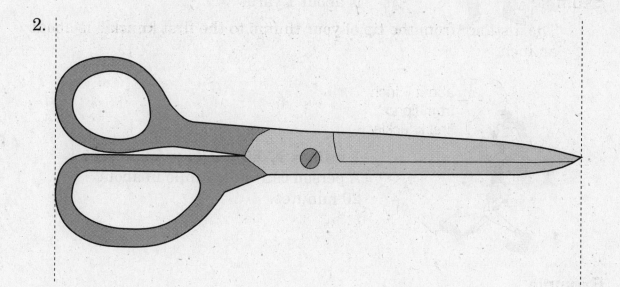

Estimate: about _____ in.   **Measurement:** _____ in.

3.

Estimate: about _____ in.   **Measurement:** _____ in.

131

Feet, Yards, and Miles

Feet (ft), **yards (yd)**, and **miles (mi)** are three U.S. customary units used to measure longer objects or distances. To measure in feet or yards, use a yardstick.

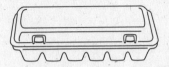

1 foot = 12 inches
A real-life egg carton is about 1 foot long.

1 yard = 3 feet = 36 inches
The distance from the top of a
real-life park bench to the ground
is about 1 yard.

1 mile = 1,760 yards = 5,280 feet
A person can walk 1 mile in about
20 minutes.

It is important to choose an appropriate unit when measuring. If you are measuring something small, choose inches. If you are measuring something large, choose feet or yards. If you are measuring long distances, choose miles.

Example

What U.S. customary unit would be **best** to measure the length of a football field? Why would you use that unit?

Since a football field is really long, **yards** would be best to measure its length. Inches and feet are too small. Miles are too large.

Practice

1. What U.S. customary unit would be **best** to measure the width of your hand?

   _____

2. What U.S. customary unit would be **best** to measure the height of your best friend?

   _____

3. What U.S. customary unit would be **best** to measure the length of a swimming pool?

   _____

4. Name some objects that are about 1 inch long.

   _____

5. Name some objects that are about 1 foot long.

   _____

6. Name some objects that are about 1 yard long.

   _____

7. Which is the **best** estimate for the length of a minivan?

   A. 2 yards

   B. 9 miles

   C. 17 feet

   D. 23 inches

8. Which is the **best** estimate for the height of a soda can?

   A. 1 mile

   B. 2 feet

   C. 4 yards

   D. 5 inches

Converting U.S. Customary Units of Length

Converting (changing) between inches, feet, yards, and miles is simple. You have to know two things: (1) how the units relate to each other, and (2) how to multiply and divide.

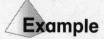 **Example**

How many feet are in 4 miles?

This question asks you to convert from a larger unit (miles) to a smaller unit (feet). When converting from a **larger** unit to a **smaller** one, you will always **multiply**.

Since you are trying to find out how many feet are in 4 miles, and there are 5,280 feet in 1 mile, you can multiply 5,280 by 4.

$$
\begin{array}{r}
\overset{1\ \ 3}{5{,}280} \leftarrow \textbf{number of feet in 1 mile} \\
\times \qquad 4 \leftarrow \textbf{number of miles} \\
\hline
21{,}120 \leftarrow \textbf{number of feet in 4 miles}
\end{array}
$$

There are 21,120 feet in 4 miles.

Example

Heidi's turtle crawled 72 inches. How many feet did the turtle crawl?

This question asks you to convert from a smaller unit (inches) to a larger unit (feet). When converting from a **smaller** unit to a **larger** one, you will always **divide**.

Since you are trying to find out how many feet equal 72 inches, and there are 12 inches in 1 foot, you can divide 72 by 12.

number of inches in 1 foot
↓
$72 \div 12 = 6 \leftarrow$ **number of feet the turtle crawled**
↑
number of inches the turtle crawled

Heidi's turtle crawled 6 feet.

Practice

1. The top of Felix's dining room table is about 12 feet long. How many yards long is Felix's table?

   Do you need to multiply or divide? _____

   In the space below, convert 12 feet to yards.

2. Jane walked 2 miles this morning. How many feet did Jane walk?

   Do you need to multiply or divide? _____

   In the space below, convert 2 miles to feet.

3. Shandra jumped 9 feet in the long jump competition. How many yards did Shandra jump?

   A. 1 yard

   B. 2 yards

   C. 3 yards

   D. 6 yards

4. Ken bought 3 feet of ribbon. How many inches of ribbon did he buy?

   A. 21 inches

   B. 24 inches

   C. 36 inches

   D. 39 inches

Metric Units of Length

Centimeters, meters, and kilometers are some of the metric units used to measure length (or distance or height). Although the United States uses the U.S. customary system, most of the world (and all scientists) use the metric system.

Centimeters

A **centimeter (cm)** is a little less than half an inch. To measure in centimeters, use a centimeter ruler.

 Example

The width of your thumb is about 1 centimeter.

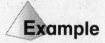

 Example

What is the length of the following crayon to the nearest centimeter?

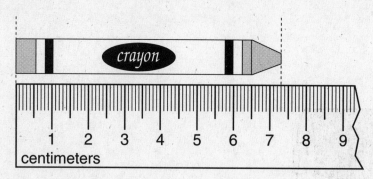

The crayon is about 7 centimeters long.

 **Practice**

Directions: For Numbers 1 through 3, estimate the length of each object to the nearest centimeter. Then measure each object with a centimeter ruler to the nearest centimeter.

1.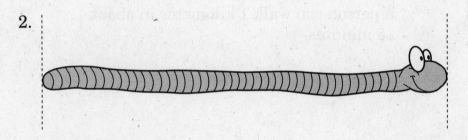

Estimate: about _____ cm   **Measurement:** _____ cm

2.

Estimate: about _____ cm   **Measurement:** _____ cm

3.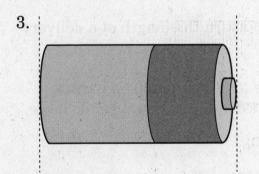

Estimate: about _____ cm   **Measurement:** _____ cm

Meters and Kilometers

Meters (m) and **kilometers (km)** are the metric units used to measure longer objects or distances. A meter is a little longer than a yard. A kilometer is a little more than half of a mile.

1 meter = 100 centimeters
A major league baseball bat is about 1 meter long.

1 kilometer = 1,000 meters
A person can walk 1 kilometer in about 15 minutes.

It is very important to choose the correct unit when measuring. Remember, the metric units of length in order from smallest to largest are centimeter, meter, and kilometer.

◢ **Example**

What metric unit would be **best** to measure the length of a delivery truck?

Meters would be best to measure the length of a delivery truck. Centimeters would be too small, and kilometers would be too large.

Practice

1. What metric unit would be **best** to measure the length of a river?

   _____

2. What metric unit would be **best** to measure the length of a car?

   _____

3. What metric unit would be **best** to measure the length of an eraser?

   _____

4. Name some objects that are about 1 centimeter long.

   _____

   _____

5. Name some objects that are about 1 meter long.

   _____

   _____

6. Which is the **best** estimate for the length of a pen?

   A. 2 kilometers

   B. 7 centimeters

   C. 12 meters

   D. 15 centimeters

7. Which is the **best** estimate for the height of an elephant?

   A. 3 meters

   B. 9 kilometers

   C. 13 centimeters

   D. 46 meters

Converting Metric Units of Length

To convert between centimeters, meters, and kilometers, you have to remember how the units relate to each other.

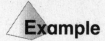**Example**

How many meters are in 3 kilometers?

You are converting from a larger unit (kilometers) to a smaller unit (meters), so you will multiply.

Since you are trying to find out how many meters are in 3 kilometers, and there are 1,000 meters in 1 kilometer, multiply 1,000 by 3.

$$
\begin{array}{r}
1{,}000 \quad \leftarrow \textbf{number of meters in 1 kilometer} \\
\underline{\times \qquad 3} \quad \leftarrow \textbf{number of kilometers} \\
3{,}000 \quad \leftarrow \textbf{number of meters in 3 kilometers}
\end{array}
$$

There are 3,000 meters in 3 kilometers.

Example

Yuki's snake is 200 centimeters long. How many meters long is the snake?

You are converting from a smaller unit (centimeters) to a larger unit (meters), so you will divide.

Since you are trying to find out how many meters equal 200 centimeters, and there are 100 centimeters in 1 meter, divide 200 by 100.

number of centimeters in 1 meter
↓
$200 \div 100 = 2$ ← **number of meters the snake is long**
↑
number of centimeters the snake is long

Yuki's snake is 2 meters long.

Objectives: M.A.3

Practice

1. Josh has a rope that is about 400 centimeters long. About how many meters long is Josh's rope?

   Do you need to multiply or divide? _____

   In the space below, convert 400 centimeters to meters.

2. The town of Mulberry is about 15 kilometers from the town of Cricket. How many meters apart are these towns?

   Do you need to multiply or divide? _____

   In the space below, convert 15 kilometers to meters.

3. Dr. Bergen is exactly 2 meters tall. How many centimeters tall is he?

   A.   2 centimeters

   B.   20 centimeters

   C.   200 centimeters

   D. 2,000 centimeters

4. Emma and Sophie walked 2,000 meters around the track at school. How many kilometers did they walk?

   A.   2 kilometers

   B.   20 kilometers

   C.   2,000 kilometers

   D. 20,000 kilometers

Mathematics Practice

1. **About** how long is the eraser?

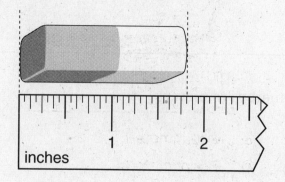

   inches

  Ⓐ $\frac{1}{2}$ inch

  Ⓑ 1 inch

  Ⓒ 1 $\frac{1}{2}$ inches

  Ⓓ 2 inches

2. Which is the **best** estimate for the distance from the floor to the ceiling in your classroom?

  Ⓐ 8 feet

  Ⓑ 9 yards

  Ⓒ 12 yards

  Ⓓ 28 inches

3. Which of the following is **best** measured in feet?

  Ⓐ the length of a pencil

  Ⓑ the thickness of a coin

  Ⓒ the depth of a swimming pool

  Ⓓ the length of a mouse

4. Which is the **best** estimate for the width of a quarter?

  Ⓐ 1 inch

  Ⓑ 1 foot

  Ⓒ 10 inches

  Ⓓ 10 feet

5. Mr. Ham is 6 feet tall. How many yards tall is Mr. Ham?

  Ⓐ 1 yard

  Ⓑ 2 yards

  Ⓒ 3 yards

  Ⓓ 12 yards

6. Which of the following is **best** measured in kilometers?

   Ⓐ the height of a person

   Ⓑ the length of an insect

   Ⓒ the length of a wall in a room

   Ⓓ the distance between two cities

7. Which is the **best** estimate for the length of a pair of scissors?

   Ⓐ 50 centimeters

   Ⓑ 50 meters

   Ⓒ 15 centimeters

   Ⓓ 15 meters

8. Which length is **shortest**?

   Ⓐ 32 inches

   Ⓑ 24 inches

   Ⓒ 3 feet

   Ⓓ 2 yards

9. Kendra's scarf is 3 feet long. How many inches long is Kendra's scarf?

   Ⓐ 12 inches

   Ⓑ 24 inches

   Ⓒ 36 inches

   Ⓓ 48 inches

10. **About** how long is the toy airplane?

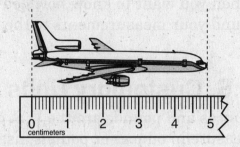

   Ⓐ 4 centimeters

   Ⓑ 5 centimeters

   Ⓒ 7 centimeters

   Ⓓ 10 centimeters

11. Sara ran 3,000 meters. How many kilometers did she run?

   Ⓐ 3 kilometers

   Ⓑ 30 kilometers

   Ⓒ 3,000 kilometers

   Ⓓ 30,000 kilometers

12. Which length is **longest**?

   Ⓐ 9 centimeters

   Ⓑ 7 centimeters

   Ⓒ 5 kilometers

   Ⓓ 4 meters

Lesson 11: Weight

When you want to know how heavy an object is, you weigh it. In this lesson, round your measurements to the nearest unit.

U.S. Customary Units of Weight

Ounces and pounds are the U.S. customary units used to measure weight. To measure in ounces or pounds, use a balance or a scale.

Ounces

Ounces (oz) are used to weigh light objects.

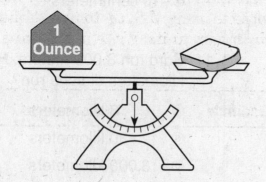

A slice of bread weighs about 1 ounce.

Pounds

Pounds (lb) are used to weigh heavier objects.

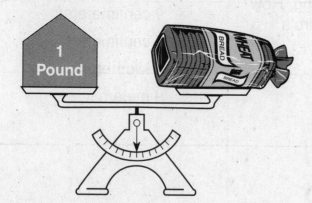

1 pound = 16 ounces
A loaf of bread weighs about 1 pound.

Objectives: M.A.1, M.A.2, M.B.1, M.B.2

It is important to use an appropriate unit when measuring. Since there are 16 ounces in a pound, an ounce is a smaller unit than a pound.

Example

What U.S. customary unit would be **best** to measure the weight of a pinecone? Why would you choose that unit?

Ounces would be best to measure the weight of a pinecone. Pounds are too large.

Practice

Directions: For Numbers 1 through 4, fill in the table with real-life objects. First estimate the weights of the objects using U.S. customary units. Then measure the weights using U.S. customary units. Write in the units you used for your measurement.

	Object	Estimate	Measurement
1.			
2.			
3.			
4.			

5. What U.S. customary unit would be **best** to measure the weight of a bicycle?

   _____

6. What U.S. customary unit would be **best** to measure the weight of a green bean?

   _____

7. What U.S. customary unit would be **best** to measure the weight of a math book?

   _____

8. Name some objects that weigh about 1 ounce.

   _____

   _____

9. Name some objects that weigh about 1 pound.

   _____

   _____

10. Which is the **best** estimate for the weight of a bag of sugar?

    A. 2 ounces

    B. 5 pounds

    C. 23 pounds

    D. 400 ounces

11. Which is the **best** estimate for the weight of a pear?

    A. 6 ounces

    B. 8 pounds

    C. 10 pounds

    D. 75 ounces

Converting U.S. Customary Units of Weight

To convert between ounces and pounds, you need to remember that there are 16 ounces in 1 pound.

 Example

How many ounces are in 2 pounds?

You are converting from a larger unit (pounds) to a smaller unit (ounces), so you will multiply.

Since you are trying to figure out how many ounces are in 2 pounds, and there are 16 ounces in 1 pound, multiply 16 by 2.

$$
\begin{array}{r}
16 \leftarrow \textbf{number of ounces in 1 pound} \\
\times\ \ 2 \leftarrow \textbf{number of pounds} \\
\hline
32 \leftarrow \textbf{number of ounces in 2 pounds}
\end{array}
$$

There are 32 ounces in 2 pounds.

Example

Mina's bunny weighs 48 ounces. How many pounds does Mina's bunny weigh?

You are converting from a smaller unit (ounces) to a larger unit (pounds), so you will divide.

Since you are trying to figure out how many pounds are equal to 48 ounces, and there are 16 ounces in a pound, divide 48 by 16.

number of ounces in one pound
$$48 \div 16 = 3 \leftarrow \textbf{number of pounds the bunny weighs}$$
number of ounces the bunny weighs

Mina's bunny weighs 3 pounds.

Practice

1. Darren bought 5 pounds of potatoes. How many ounces of potatoes did Darren buy?

   Do you need to multiply or divide? _____

   In the space below, convert 5 pounds to ounces.

2. Rory's baby brother weighed 96 ounces at birth. How many pounds did he weigh?

   Do you need to multiply or divide? _____

   In the space below, convert 96 ounces to pounds.

3. Jill bought a pumpkin that weighs 8 pounds. How many ounces does the pumpkin weigh?

   A. 60 ounces

   B. 112 ounces

   C. 128 ounces

   D. 144 ounces

4. Paul's puppy weighs 112 ounces. How many pounds does the puppy weigh?

   A. 6 pounds

   B. 7 pounds

   C. 8 pounds

   D. 9 pounds

Metric Units of Weight

Grams and kilograms are the metric units used to measure weight.

Grams

Grams (g) are used to weigh light objects.

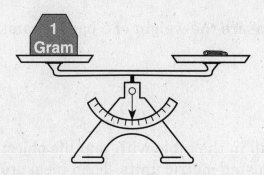

A paper clip weighs about 1 gram.

Kilograms

Kilograms (kg) are used to weigh heavier objects. A kilogram is a little more than 2 pounds.

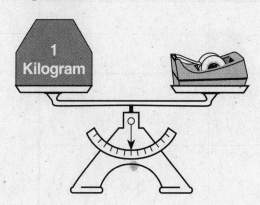

1 kilogram = 1,000 grams
A tape dispenser weighs about
1 kilogram.

It is important to use an appropriate unit when measuring. Since there are 1,000 grams in a kilogram, a gram is a smaller unit than a kilogram.

Example

What metric unit would be **best** to measure the weight of a baby? Why would you choose that unit?

Kilograms would be best to measure the weight of a baby. Grams are too small.

Practice

Directions: For Numbers 1 through 4, fill in the table with real-life objects. First estimate the weights of the objects using metric units. Then measure the weights using metric units. Write in the units you used for your measurement.

	Object	Estimate	Measurement
1.			
2.			
3.			
4.			

5. What metric unit would be **best** to measure the weight of a leaf?

_____

6. What metric unit would be **best** to measure the weight of a dictionary?

_____

7. What metric unit would be **best** to measure the weight of a watermelon?

_____

8. Name some objects that weigh about 1 gram.

_____

_____

9. Name some objects that weigh about 1 kilogram.

_____

_____

10. Which is the **best** estimate for the weight of a feather?

   A. 1 gram

   B. 4 kilograms

   C. 15 kilograms

   D. 300 grams

11. Which is the **best** estimate for the weight of a horse?

   A. 2 kilograms

   B. 12 grams

   C. 145 grams

   D. 450 kilograms

Converting Metric Units of Weight

To convert between grams and kilograms, you need to remember that there are 1,000 grams in 1 kilogram.

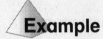 **Example**

How many grams are in 4 kilograms?

You are converting from a larger unit (kilograms) to a smaller unit (grams), so you will multiply.

Since you are trying to figure out how many grams are in 4 kilograms, and there are 1,000 grams in 1 kilogram, multiply 1,000 by 4.

$$
\begin{array}{r}
1,000 \leftarrow \textbf{number of grams in 1 kilogram} \\
\times \quad\quad 4 \leftarrow \textbf{number of kilograms} \\
\hline
4,000 \leftarrow \textbf{number of grams in 4 kilograms}
\end{array}
$$

There are 4,000 grams in 4 kilograms.

Example

Mrs. Freeman's purse weighs 2,000 grams. How many kilograms does her purse weigh?

You are converting from a smaller unit (grams) to a larger unit (kilograms), so you will divide.

Since you are trying to figure out how many kilograms are in 2,000 grams, and there are 1,000 grams in 1 kilogram, divide 2,000 by 1,000.

number of grams in 1 kilogram
↓
$2,000 \div 1,000 = 2 \leftarrow$ **number of kilograms the purse weighs**
↑
number of grams the purse weighs

Mrs. Freeman's purse weighs 2 kilograms.

Practice

1. John told the woman behind the deli counter that he wanted 2 kilograms of Swiss cheese. How many grams of cheese did he want?

   Do you need to multiply or divide? _____

   In the space below, convert 2 kilograms to grams.

2. Sarah caught a fish that weighed 8,000 grams. How many kilograms did the fish weigh?

   Do you need to multiply or divide? _____

   In the space below, convert 8,000 grams to kilograms.

3. Karen's camping gear weighs 6,000 grams. How many kilograms does Karen's camping gear weigh?

   A. 600 kilograms

   B. 60 kilograms

   C. 6 kilograms

   D. 0.6 kilograms

4. A miner found 1 kilogram of gold. How many grams of gold did the miner find?

   A. 10,000 grams

   B. 1,000 grams

   C. 100 grams

   D. 10 grams

Mathematics Practice

1. Which real-life object weighs about 1 pound?

   Ⓐ

   Ⓑ

   Ⓒ

   Ⓓ

2. Valerie's backpack weighs 80 ounces. How many pounds does Valerie's backpack weigh?

   Ⓐ 7 pounds

   Ⓑ 6 pounds

   Ⓒ 5 pounds

   Ⓓ 4 pounds

3. Which is the **best** estimate for the weight of a real-life cat?

   Ⓐ 4 kilograms

   Ⓑ 40 kilograms

   Ⓒ 400 kilograms

   Ⓓ 4,000 kilograms

4. Jackie works at an ice cream shop. Each Super Sundae is supposed to weigh 1 pound with ice cream and toppings. Jackie adds ice cream weighing 14 ounces. How many ounces of toppings should she add to make it weigh 1 pound?

   Ⓐ 1 ounce

   Ⓑ 2 ounces

   Ⓒ 10 ounces

   Ⓓ 20 ounces

5. Ryan's lizard weighs 7 kilograms. How many grams does the lizard weigh?

Ⓐ   7 grams

Ⓑ   70 grams

Ⓒ   700 grams

Ⓓ 7,000 grams

6. How much do the oranges weigh?

Ⓐ 14 ounces

Ⓑ 12 ounces

Ⓒ 10 ounces

Ⓓ   8 ounces

7. Which weight is the **heaviest**?

Ⓐ 1,000 grams

Ⓑ 5 grams

Ⓒ 3 kilograms

Ⓓ 1 kilogram

8. How much does the book weigh?

Ⓐ 1 kilogram

Ⓑ 2 kilograms

Ⓒ 3 kilograms

Ⓓ 4 kilograms

9. Which of the following objects would you **most likely** weigh in grams?

Ⓐ a gumball

Ⓑ a shark

Ⓒ a table

Ⓓ a lawn mower

Lesson 12: Capacity

When you measure how much liquid you have in a container, you are measuring **capacity**. In this lesson, round your measurements to the nearest unit.

U.S. Customary Units of Capacity

Cups, pints, quarts, and gallons are the U.S. customary units used to measure capacity.

Cups, Pints, Quarts, and Gallons

Cups (c) are used to measure small amounts of liquid. Use **pints (pt)**, **quarts (qt)**, and **gallons (gal)** to measure larger amounts of liquid. To measure capacity, use a measuring cup.

A small milk carton has a capacity of 1 cup.

1 pint = 2 cups
A small ice cream container has a capacity of 1 pint.

1 quart = 2 pints = 4 cups
A bottle of cleaner has a capacity of 1 quart.

1 gallon = 4 quarts
A milk container has a capacity of 1 gallon.

It is important to use an appropriate unit when measuring.

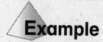 **Example**

What U.S. customary unit would be **best** to measure the capacity of a swimming pool? Why would you choose that unit?

Gallons would be best to measure the capacity of a swimming pool. Cups, pints, and quarts are all too small.

Practice

Directions: For Numbers 1 through 4, fill in the table with real-life containers. First estimate the capacities of the containers using U.S. customary units. Then measure their capacities using U.S. customary units. Write in the units you used for your measurement.

	Container	Estimate	Measurement
1.			
2.			
3.			
4.			

5. What U.S. customary unit would be **best** to measure the capacity of water in a drinking class?

_____

6. What U.S. customary unit would be **best** to measure the capacity of oil in a large barrel?

_____

7. Which is the **best** estimate for the capacity of a coffee mug?

A. 1 quart

B. 2 cups

C. 3 pints

D. 4 gallons

8. Which is the **best** estimate for the capacity of a kitchen sink?

A. 4 pints

B. 5 quarts

C. 6 gallons

D. 7 cups

Converting U.S. Customary Units of Capacity

To convert from one unit of capacity to another, you need to remember how the units relate to each other.

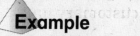 **Example**

How many quarts are in 10 gallons?

You are converting from a larger unit (gallons) to a smaller unit (quarts), so you will multiply.

Since you are trying to figure out how many quarts are in 10 gallons, and there are 4 quarts in 1 gallon, multiply 10 by 4.

$$
\begin{array}{r}
10 \leftarrow \textbf{number of gallons} \\
\times\ \ 4 \leftarrow \textbf{number of quarts in 1 gallon} \\
\hline
40 \leftarrow \textbf{number of quarts in 10 gallons}
\end{array}
$$

There are 40 quarts in 10 gallons.

Example

Fran drank 6 cups of milk. How many pints did she drink?

You are converting from a smaller unit (cups) to a larger unit (pints), so you will divide.

Since you are trying to figure out how many pints there are in 6 cups, and there are 2 cups in 1 pint, divide 6 by 2.

number of cups in 1 pint
↓
$6 \div 2 = 3 \leftarrow$ **number of pints of milk Fran drank**
↑
number of cups of milk Fran drank

Fran drank 3 pints of milk.

Practice

1. A jug of apple juice contains 12 pints. How many quarts of apple juice are in the jug?

   Do you need to multiply or divide? _____

   In the space below, convert 12 pints to quarts.

2. Mrs. Malloy's punch recipe calls for 5 pints of ginger ale. How many cups of ginger ale are in the punch?

   Do you need to multiply or divide? _____

   In the space below, convert 5 pints to cups.

3. Farmer Ted's goat produces 6 gallons of milk each week. How many quarts of milk does the goat produce?

   A. 12 quarts

   B. 18 quarts

   C. 24 quarts

   D. 30 quarts

4. Ms. Gonzales has 24 students in her third-grade class. Each student drinks 1 cup of milk at lunch. How many pints of milk do the students drink altogether?

   A. 12 pints

   B. 16 pints

   C. 24 pints

   D. 48 pints

Metric Units of Capacity

Milliliters and liters are two of the metric units used to measure capacity.

Milliliters

Milliliters (mL) are used to measure small amounts of liquid.

A real-life medicine dropper holds about
1 milliliter.

Liters

Liters (L) are used to measure larger amounts of liquid. A liter is a little more than 1 quart.

1 liter = 1,000 milliliters
An orange juice container holds about 1 liter.

It is important to use an appropriate unit when measuring. Since there are 1,000 milliliters in a liter, a milliliter is a smaller unit than a liter.

Example

What metric unit would be **best** to measure the capacity of a water glass? Why would you choose that unit?

Milliliters would be best to measure the capacity of a water glass. Liters are too large.

Practice

Directions: For Numbers 1 through 4, fill in the table with real-life containers. First estimate the capacities of the containers using metric units. Then measure the capacities using metric units. Write in the units you used for your measurement.

	Container	Estimate	Measurement
1.			
2.			
3.			
4.			

5. What metric unit would be **best** to measure the capacity of a can of soup?

_____

6. What metric unit would be **best** to measure the capacity of a gas can?

_____

7. Which is the **best** estimate for the capacity of a large bottle of liquid laundry soap?

A. 4 liters

B. 40 milliliters

C. 40 liters

D. 400 milliliters

8. Which is the **best** estimate for the capacity of a can of soda?

A. 35 milliliters

B. 350 liters

C. 350 milliliters

D. 3,500 liters

Converting Metric Units of Capacity

To convert between milliliters and liters, remember there are 1,000 milliliters in a liter.

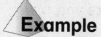

Example

How many milliliters are in 3 liters?

You are converting from a larger unit (liters) to a smaller unit (milliliters), so you will multiply.

Since you are trying to figure out how many milliliters are in 3 liters, and there are 1,000 milliliters in 1 liter, multiply 3 by 1,000.

$$
\begin{array}{r}
1,000 \leftarrow \textbf{number of milliliters in 1 liter} \\
\times \qquad 3 \leftarrow \textbf{number of liters} \\
\hline
3,000 \leftarrow \textbf{number of milliliters in 3 liters}
\end{array}
$$

There are 3,000 milliliters in 3 liters.

Example

Chris drank 2,000 milliliters of water today. How many liters of water did he drink?

You are converting from a smaller unit (milliliters) to a larger unit (liters), so you will divide.

Since you are trying to figure out how many liters are in 2,000 milliliters, and there are 1,000 milliliters in 1 liter, divide 2,000 by 1,000.

number of milliliters in 1 liter
↓
$2,000 \div 1,000 = 2$ ← **number of liters of water Chris drank**
↑
number of milliliters of water Chris drank

Chris drank 2 liters of water.

Practice

1. Jada's mom bought a 2-liter bottle of juice for Jada's birthday party. How many milliliters of juice are in the bottle?

   Do you need to multiply or divide? _____

   In the space below, convert 2 liters to milliliters.

2. Maya's bathroom sink holds 8,000 milliliters of water. How many liters does Maya's sink hold?

   Do you need to multiply or divide? _____

   In the space below, convert 8,000 milliliters to liters.

3. Sean handed out 1-liter bottles of orange juice after the soccer game. How many milliliters of juice were in each bottle?

   A. 1 milliliter

   B. 20 milliliters

   C. 200 milliliters

   D. 1,000 milliliters

4. Megan measured $\frac{1}{2}$ liter of water. How many milliliters of water is this?

   A. 20 milliliters

   B. 50 milliliters

   C. 500 milliliters

   D. 2,000 milliliters

Mathematics Practice

1. Which real-life object **most likely** holds 2 gallons?

    Ⓐ

    Ⓑ

    Ⓒ

    Ⓓ

2. How many cups are in 1 gallon?

    Ⓐ 32 cups

    Ⓑ 16 cups

    Ⓒ 8 cups

    Ⓓ 4 cups

3. Which unit of measurement would you **most likely** use to measure the amount of hot cocoa in a mug?

    Ⓐ cups

    Ⓑ quarts

    Ⓒ pints

    Ⓓ gallons

4. Which container has the **least** capacity?

    Ⓐ
    1 cup

    Ⓑ
    1 quart

    Ⓒ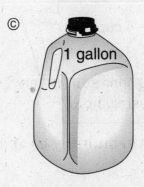
    1 gallon

    Ⓓ
    1 pint

165

5. Which unit of measurement would you **most likely** use to measure the amount of water in a full bathtub?

   Ⓐ cups

   Ⓑ quarts

   Ⓒ pints

   Ⓓ gallons

6. How much liquid is in the measuring cup?

   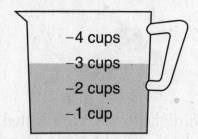

   Ⓐ 1 cup

   Ⓑ 2 cups

   Ⓒ 3 cups

   Ⓓ 4 cups

7. Which real-life object would **most likely** have a capacity of 15 milliliters?

   Ⓐ glass of juice

   Ⓑ bottle of shampoo

   Ⓒ bowl of soup

   Ⓓ bottle of nail polish

8. How many milliliters are in 10 liters?

   Ⓐ   1 milliliter

   Ⓑ   100 milliliters

   Ⓒ   1,000 milliliters

   Ⓓ 10,000 milliliters

9. Which measurement is the **greatest**?

   Ⓐ 40 liters of soda

   Ⓑ 100 liters of water

   Ⓒ 200 milliliters of orange juice

   Ⓓ 500 milliliters of seawater

10. Which tool would you use to measure the amount of liquid in a water bottle?

    Ⓐ measuring cup

    Ⓑ ruler

    Ⓒ scale

    Ⓓ tape measure

11. How many pints are in 3 quarts?

    Ⓐ 2

    Ⓑ 4

    Ⓒ 6

    Ⓓ 8

Lesson 13: Time and Temperature

Time tells you what part of the day it is or how long it takes for an event to occur. **Temperature** is the measure of how hot or cold something is.

Time

Time is measured using a clock. Clocks measure time in hours and minutes.

This is a **digital clock**.

Hour   Minutes

This is an **analog clock**.

Each day has 24 hours. The 12 hours from midnight to noon are called the A.M. hours. The 12 hours from noon to midnight are called the P.M. hours. A digital clock usually has a little light beside the time that shows whether it is A.M. or P.M. An analog clock does not show whether it is A.M. or P.M.

The short hand of the analog clock points to the hours. The numbers around the clock show the hours. The long hand points to the minutes. The little marks around the clock show the minutes. It takes 5 minutes for the long hand to move from one number to the next. There are 60 seconds in one minute. There are 60 minutes in one hour. This clock shows 8:15.

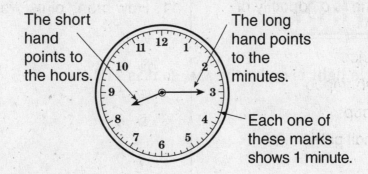

The short hand points to the hours.

The long hand points to the minutes.

Each one of these marks shows 1 minute.

If it is between midnight and noon, it would be 8:15 A.M. If it is between noon and midnight, it would be 8:15 P.M.

Unit 4 – *Measurement*

Objectives: M.A.1, M.A.2, M.B.1

Example

What time is it? It is between noon and midnight.

The short hand shows the hours. It is between the 5 and 6, so the hour is 5.

The long hand shows the minutes. It is between the 9 and 10. Because each number represents 5 minutes, multiply 5 and 9 and then add the number of marks past the 9 until you get to the long hand. It is 3 marks past the 9.

$$5 \times 9 = 45$$

$$45 + 3 = 48$$

Because it is between noon and midnight, it is 5:48 P.M.

Example

What time is it?

The little light is on by the A.M., so it is 11:14 A.M.

Practice

Directions: For Numbers 1 through 7, write the time shown on the clock. Be sure to include A.M. or P.M.

1. It is between noon and midnight.

_____

2. It is between midnight and noon.

_____

3. It is between midnight and noon.

_____

4.

_____

5.

_____

6.

_____

7.

_____

Elapsed Time

Elapsed time is the time that has passed between two events.

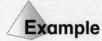**Example**

Jamie went outside at 10:35 A.M. She came back inside at 11:15 A.M. How long was Jamie outside?

Jamie was outside less than an hour. Count the minutes by skip counting by 5's.

10:35	10:40	10:45	10:50	10:55	11:00	11:05	11:10	11:15
	5	10	15	20	25	30	35	40

Jamie was outside for 40 minutes.

Example

Frankie gets done with lunch at school at 12:10 P.M. School gets out at 3:20 P.M. How long is it from the end of Frankie's lunch until school gets out?

Count the hours first. Then count the minutes.

12:10	1:10	2:10	3:10		3:10	3:15	3:20
	1	2	3			5	10

It is 3 hours, 10 minutes from the end of Frankie's lunch until school gets out.

Practice

1. Leena's family left their house at 8:00 A.M. to drive to the beach. They arrived at the beach at 1:30 P.M.

How long did it take for Leena's family to drive from their house to the beach?

_____

2. On Saturday morning, Michelle played soccer. The clock on the left shows the time she went to the soccer game.

She returned home 2 hours, 25 minutes later. Draw the hands on the blank clock on the right to show the time Michelle returned home. Then write the time on the line. Be sure to include A.M. or P.M.

_____

3. Tim has to be at school in 1 hour, 50 minutes. It is 6:40 A.M. now. Circle the clock that shows the time Tim needs to be at school.

4. Jamal started his homework at 3:25 P.M. He finished his homework at 4:40 P.M.

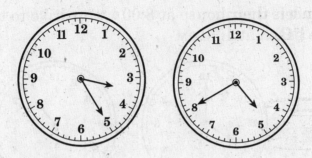

How long did it take Jamal to do his homework? _____

Directions: Use the information below to answer Numbers 5 and 6.

Mrs. Abbot's class is working on science projects at home. The table below shows how long each student has spent working on his or her science project.

Time Spent on Science Project

Student	Time Spent
Alexander	2 hours
Brittany	250 minutes
Carl	4 hours
Desmond	180 minutes

5. Who has spent the **most** time on his or her science project?

_____

6. Who has spent the **least** time on his or her science project?

_____

Temperature

Temperature is measured in degrees using a thermometer. The U.S. customary unit is **degrees Fahrenheit (°F)**. The metric unit is **degrees Celsius (°C)**.

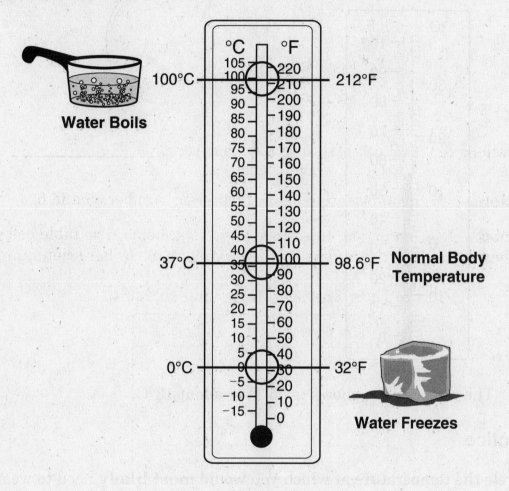

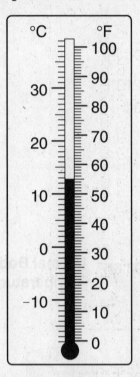

Example

What temperature is shown on the thermometer? Write the temperature in both °F and °C.

The temperature shown is 55°F, or about 13°C.

Practice

1. Circle the temperature at which you would **most likely** need to wear a jacket.

   40°F   72°F   90°F

2. One summer day, Steve saw a bank thermometer that read 35°. It was really warm outside. Did the thermometer measure in degrees Celsius or degrees Fahrenheit?

   _____

3. It was 75°F at noon. When Austin went to bed, the temperature had dropped 16°F. What was the temperature when Austin went to bed?

   _____

Directions: For Numbers 4 through 7, write the temperature shown on each thermometer in both °F and °C.

4.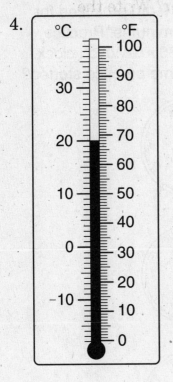

_____ °F

_____ °C

6.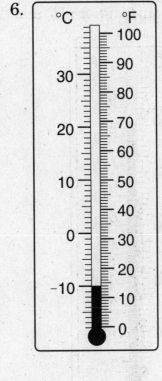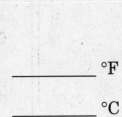

_____ °F

_____ °C

5.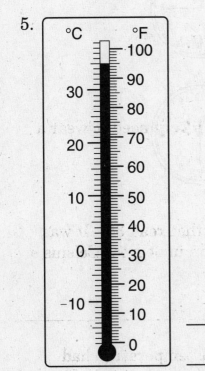

_____ °F

_____ °C

7.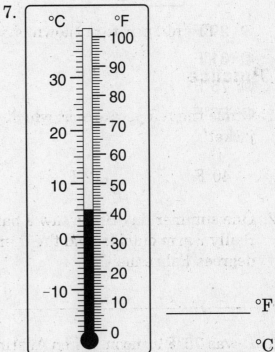

_____ °F

_____ °C

Mathematics Practice

1. What temperature does the thermometer show, in °F?

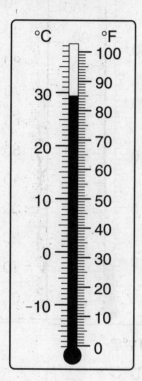

- Ⓐ 29°F
- Ⓑ 31°F
- Ⓒ 75°F
- Ⓓ 85°F

2. The football team practiced for 2 hours, 15 minutes. Practice ended at 1:30 P.M. Which clock shows the time practice started?

Ⓐ

Ⓑ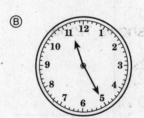

Ⓒ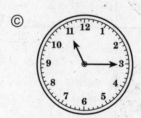

Ⓓ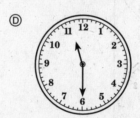

3. What time does the digital clock show?

Ⓐ 1:52 P.M.

Ⓑ 1:52 A.M.

Ⓒ 2:51 P.M.

Ⓓ 2:51 A.M.

4. Which clock shows 12:08?

Ⓐ

Ⓑ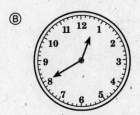

Ⓒ

Ⓓ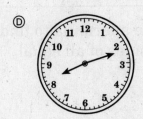

5. What temperature does the thermometer show, in °C?

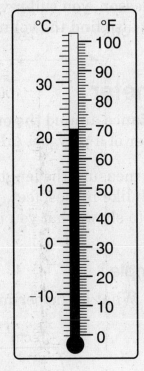

Ⓐ 19°C

Ⓑ 21°C

Ⓒ 25°C

Ⓓ 39°C

6. What time does the digital clock show?

Ⓐ 7:03 P.M.

Ⓑ 7:30 P.M.

Ⓒ 7:03 A.M.

Ⓓ 7:30 A.M.

Lesson 14: Geometric Measurement

In this lesson, you will review how to find the perimeter and area of polygons. You will also find the volume of rectangular prisms.

Perimeter

The distance around the outside of a polygon is the **perimeter**. To find the perimeter of a polygon, **add the lengths of all the sides** of the polygon.

You can measure the lengths of the sides of the figure using standard units of length like inches, feet, yards, centimeters, or meters. Be sure to label your answer to show what you used for your unit.

 Example

What is the perimeter of the following quadrilateral?

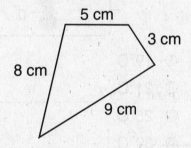

Add the lengths of all the sides of the quadrilateral.

$5 + 3 + 9 + 8 = 25$

The perimeter of the quadrilateral is 25 cm.

Formula for Perimeter

A **formula** is a type of open number sentence. You can use a formula to find the perimeter (*P*) of regular polygons. For polygons with sides of all equal lengths, use this formula:

$$P = n \times s$$

P is the perimeter, *n* is the number of sides of the polygon, and *s* is the length of a side. Used correctly, formulas will always get you the right answer.

Example

What is the perimeter of the following equilateral triangle?

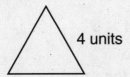

4 units

There are 3 sides of the same length, so use the following formula.

$P = 3 \times s$

Each side has a length of 4 units, so substitute 4 for *s*.

$P = 3 \times 4$

$= 12$

The perimeter of the triangle is 12 units.

Practice

1. Tony's yard is shown below. What is the perimeter? _____

15 yd

8 yd   8 yd

15 yd

2. Darby's playpen is shown below. What is the perimeter? _____

10 ft

8 ft   8 ft

6 ft

Directions: Use the figure and formula to answer Numbers 3 through 5.

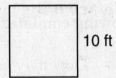

10 ft

$P = 4 \times s$

3. Explain what each term in the formula stands for.

   P _____

   4 _____

   s _____

4. What goes in place of the s in the formula? _____

5. What is the perimeter of the figure? _____

Directions: The pentagon below has sides that are all the same length. Use the pentagon to answer Numbers 6 through 8.

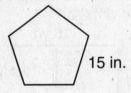

15 in.

6. Write a formula you can use to find the perimeter of the pentagon.

   _____

7. Explain what each letter and number in the formula means.

   _____

   _____

   _____

8. What is the perimeter of the pentagon? _____

Objectives: M.B.4

Area

The **area** of a polygon is the number of **square units** needed to cover the surface of the polygon.

The square units you use can be of any size. They may be squares that are 1 inch, 1 foot, 1 yard, 1 centimeter, or 1 meter on a side. Or they can be any other length as long as they are square.

Example

What is the area of this square?

= 1 square unit

Count the number of square units that make up the square. There are 4.

The area of the square is 4 square units.

Example

What is the area of this polygon?

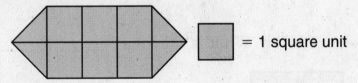
= 1 square unit

Count the number of whole square units that make up the polygon. There are 6.

Count the number of partial square units that make up the polygon. How many whole square units can be made from the partial square units? There are 4 partial square units, which can make 2 whole square units.

Add to find the total number of whole square units that make up the figure.

$$6 + 2 = 8$$

The area of the polygon is 8 square units.

Formula for Area

You can use this formula to find the area (*A*) of a rectangle:

$$A = l \times w$$

A is the area, *l* is the length, and *w* is the width. Multiply the length times the width. When you multiply units, the product is in square units.

Example

Find the area of the following rectangle.

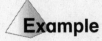

3 units

9 units

Multiply the length times the width to find the area of the rectangle.

$$A = 9 \times 3$$
$$= 27$$

The area of the rectangle is 27 square units.

Practice

1. Randall's book is shown below. What is the area? _____

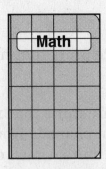

Math

KEY

☐ = 1 square inch

2. A CD case is shown below. What is the area? _____

Rock Music

KEY

☐ = 1 square inch

Directions: For Numbers 3 through 6, find the area of each polygon in square units.

3.

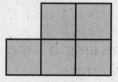

$A =$ _____ square units

4.

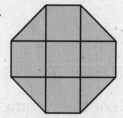

$A =$ _____ square units

5.

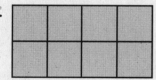

$A =$ _____ square units

6.

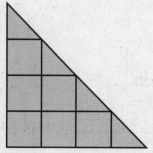

$A =$ _____ square units

Directions: For Numbers 7 through 10, find the area of each rectangle in square units.

7.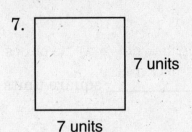

7 units

7 units

$A =$ _____ square units

8.

4 units

4 units

$A =$ _____ square units

9.

3 units

7 units

$A =$ _____ square units

10.

1 unit

10 units

$A =$ _____ square units

Volume

The **volume** of a solid figure is the number of **cubic units** needed to fill the solid figure.

The cubic units you use can be cubes with any side length. They may be cubes with side lengths of 1 inch, 1 foot, 1 yard, 1 centimeter, or 1 meter.

 Example

What is the volume of this cube?

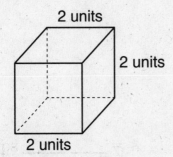

Fill the cube with cubic units to help you find the volume.

Each cubic unit 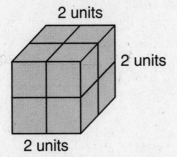 is 1 unit long, 1 unit wide, and 1 unit high.

2 units

2 units

2 units

Remember to count the cubic units that you cannot see.

The volume of the cube is 8 cubic units.

Practice

Directions: For Numbers 1 through 4, find the volume of each rectangular prism in cubic units.

1.

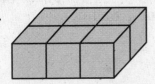

V = _____ cubic units

2.

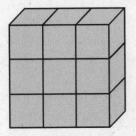

V = _____ cubic units

3.

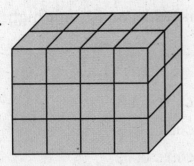

V = _____ cubic units

4.

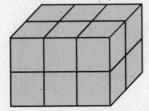

V = _____ cubic units

Mathematics Practice

1. Sheila and her parents want to put a fence around the vegetable garden. How many meters of fencing will they need?

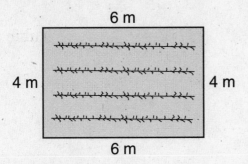

6 m

4 m　　4 m

6 m

Ⓐ 20 meters

Ⓑ 24 meters

Ⓒ 28 meters

Ⓓ 30 meters

2. Bryan's parents are putting a tile floor in their hallway. Each tile is 1 square foot. How many tiles will it take to complete the floor?

4 ft

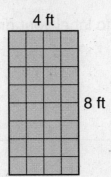

8 ft

Ⓐ 12

Ⓑ 32

Ⓒ 36

Ⓓ 40

3. The sides of the hexagon below are all the same length. Which formula could be used to find the perimeter of the hexagon?

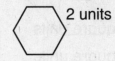

2 units

Ⓐ $P = 2 \times 2$

Ⓑ $P = 6 + 2$

Ⓒ $P = 6 + 6$

Ⓓ $P = 6 \times 2$

4. What is the volume of this cube?

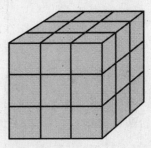

Ⓐ 9 cubic units

Ⓑ 27 cubic units

Ⓒ 36 cubic units

Ⓓ 54 cubic units

5. What is the area of this polygon?

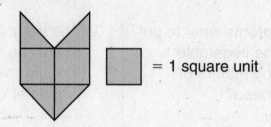

= 1 square unit

Ⓐ 2 square units

Ⓑ 3 square units

Ⓒ 4 square units

Ⓓ 6 square units

6. Daniel's deck is shown below.

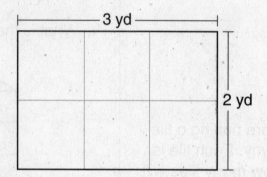

Part A

What is the perimeter of Daniel's deck? Be sure to label your answer with the correct units.

Part B

What is the area of Daniel's deck? Be sure to label your answer with the correct units.

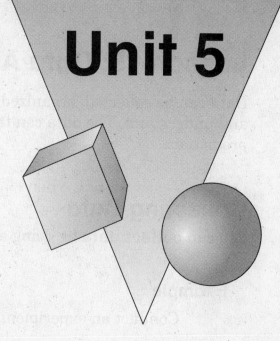

Unit 5

Data Analysis and Probability

Have you ever seen a chart or graph in the newspaper or on TV? These are tools that people use to show a lot of information at the same time. Tables and graphs are used to compare data.

Have you ever flipped a coin a number of times, kept track of the outcomes, and then used the results to predict the next outcome? This is a way of determining and using probability.

In this unit, you will organize, interpret, compare, and display data. You will determine the median, mode, and range of data. You will also describe the probability of an event.

In This Unit

Data Analysis

Probability

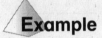

Lesson 15: Data Analysis

Data can be collected, organized, and displayed so that they are easy to read and understand. The data can then be used to draw conclusions or make predictions.

Collecting Data

You can **collect data** by doing an experiment.

 Example

Conduct an experiment to see where the spinner stops most often.

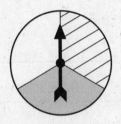

The spinner was spun 15 times. Here are the results:

gray, striped, white, white, gray, striped, striped, white, white, gray, striped, gray, striped, gray, gray

You can also collect data by asking people questions. This is called taking a **survey**.

Example

Jimmy asked the other third graders this survey question: "What is your favorite lunch?" Here are the answers that were given:

hot dogs, pizza, soup, spaghetti, pizza, chili, hot dogs, soup, hamburgers, pizza, hot dogs, soup, hamburgers, spaghetti, soup, pizza, pizza, hamburgers, pizza, soup

Practice

1. Conduct an experiment to see which number on a number cube numbered 1 through 6 occurs most often when rolled. Roll a number cube 20 times. Write down the number that you roll each time.

_____

_____

_____

2. Ask your classmates the following survey question: "What is your favorite color?" Write down the colors that your classmates give.

_____

_____

_____

3. Think of your own survey question. Write it on the following lines.

_____

_____

_____

Now ask your classmates your survey question. Write down your results on the following lines.

_____

_____

_____

Median, Mode, and Range

Median, mode, and range each use a number to describe a set of numbers (data). The **median** is the number that is in the middle of a set. To find the median, order the numbers from the least value to the greatest value.

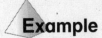 **Example**

The following data set shows the number of birdies Mr. Jackson got during each of the last five weeks while playing golf.

4, 5, 1, 2, 5

To find the median, write the numbers in order from least to greatest.

1, 2, **4**, 5, 5

The median (middle number) of this data set is 4.

The **mode** is the number that appears most often in a set.

Example

Find the mode of Mr. Jackson's data.

To find the mode, look for the number that appears the most.

4, **5**, 1, 2, **5**

The mode of this data set is 5.

The **range** tells you the difference between the largest number in the set and the smallest number in the set.

Example

Find the range of Mr. Jackson's data.

To find the range, subtract the smallest number in the set (1) from the largest number in the set (5): 5 − 1 = 4

The range of this data set is 4.

Practice

Directions: Use the following information to answer Numbers 1 through 3.

Tasha went fishing each day last week. The following list shows how many fish she caught each day.

5, 7, 4, 6, 7, 3, 9

1. What is the **median** of the data? _____

2. What is the **mode** of the data? _____

3. What is the **range** of the data? _____

Directions: Use the following information to answer Numbers 4 through 6.

The table shows how many students participated in two school activities last week.

Day	Dodgeball	Swimming
Monday	9	5
Tuesday	8	4
Wednesday	5	8
Thursday	9	4
Friday	4	9

4. What is the **median** of the students who participated in swimming?

_____

5. What is the **mode** of the students who participated in dodgeball?

_____

6. What is the **range** of the students who participated in dodgeball?

_____

Organizing and Displaying Data

Once you have collected your data, it is important to **organize** and **display** them so that they can be used. The lists in the spinner experiment and survey question examples are fine, but they are hard to use. Charts and graphs display the data so they are easier to use. The title of the chart or graph will give you the main idea of the data that are represented in the chart or graph. The labels tell you what each column or row represents.

Tally Charts

A **tally chart** is an easy way to organize and display your data. The tally marks show the number of times that each value occurs.

 **Example**

Here is the tally chart for Jimmy's survey question from page 190.

Third Graders' Favorite Lunches

title ⟶

label ⟶

Type of Lunch	Number of Students	
Pizza	卌 I	6
Hot dogs	III	3
Chili	I	1
Spaghetti	II	2
Hamburgers	III	3
Soup	卌	5

⟵ label

KEY
I = 1
卌 = 5

➤ **TIP:** Look for the row with the most tallies to find the **mode** on a tally chart.

Practice

Directions: Use the tally chart from the previous page to answer Numbers 1 through 3.

1. How many of the third graders said that soup is their favorite lunch?

   _____

2. What did the least number of third graders say was their favorite lunch?

   _____

3. What two things did exactly 3 third graders say was their favorite lunch?

   _____

Directions: For Numbers 4 through 6, use the data you collected in the number cube experiment on page 191.

4. Make a tally chart of the data.

5. Which numbers, if any, occurred the same number of times?

   _____

6. What is the mode of the data? _____

Directions: For Numbers 7 through 9, use the data you collected in the favorite color survey on page 191.

7. Make a tally chart of the data.

8. Which colors, if any, did the same number of students say were their favorite?

_____

9. Put the colors in order, starting with the color that the greatest number of students said was their favorite and ending with the color that the least number of students said was their favorite.

_____

_____

Bar Graphs

A **bar graph** uses thick bars to compare information. The bars can go up and down or left and right. Be sure to check the labels on the graph.

Example

The third graders at Lucas Elementary collected newspapers during the school year. This bar graph shows how many pounds of newspapers the third graders collected each month.

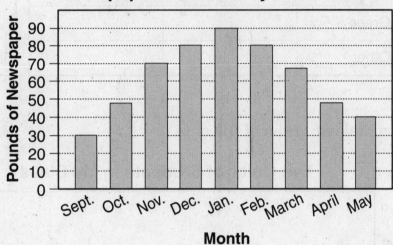

Practice

Directions: Use the bar graph above to answer Numbers 1 through 4.

1. How many pounds of newspaper were collected in December? _____

2. During which month was the most newspaper collected?

_____

3. What is the label along the side of the graph?

_____

4. What is the label along the bottom of the graph?

_____

Directions: Collect data about the eye color of your classmates. Then use the data to answer Numbers 5 through 7.

5. Fill in this tally chart with your data.

Eye Color of Students in My Class

Color of Eyes	Number of Students	
Brown		
Blue		
Green		
Other		

KEY

| = 1

𝗜𝗜𝗜𝗜𝗜 = 5

6. Make a horizontal bar graph of the data.

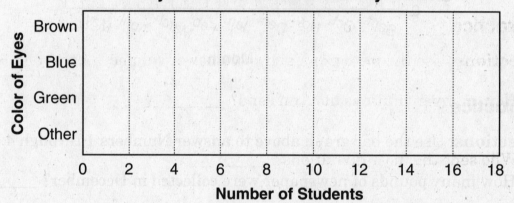

Eye Color of Students in My Class

7. If you picked a student from your class at random, what do you think his or her eye color would be? Explain your answer.

_____

_____

Pictographs

A **pictograph** uses pictures to show data. Use the **KEY** to help you figure out the number of times that each value or result from the pictograph occurs.

Example

Three students are in charge of sending out invitations for a class party. The following pictograph shows the number of invitations Ty, Ann, and Zoe sent to their classmates.

Invitations Sent to Classmates

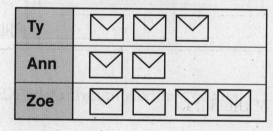

KEY

☑ = 2 invitations sent

Practice

Directions: Use the pictograph above to answer Numbers 1 through 5.

1. How many invitations did Ann send? _____

2. Who sent the most invitations? _____

3. How many invitations were sent altogether? _____

4. How many more invitations did Zoe send than Ty? _____

5. Write your own question about the pictograph.

_____

_____

Directions: Conduct an experiment to see which sides land up when 2 coins are flipped in the air at the same time. Flip the coins 25 times. Then use the data to answer Numbers 6 through 10.

6. Fill in the following tally chart with the data.

Coin Flip Experiment

Outcome	Number of Occurrences	
2 Heads		
2 Tails		
1 Head, 1 Tail		

7. Make a pictograph of the data. Use the symbols found in the KEY in your pictograph.

Coin Flip Experiment

2 Heads	
2 Tails	
1 Head, 1 Tail	

KEY
◖ = 2 occurrences
◖ = 1 occurrence

8. How many times did the coins both land heads up? _____

9. Which outcome occurred the **greatest** number of times? _____

10. If you flip the coins one more time, what outcome do you think will occur? Explain your answer.

_____

_____

Line Plots

A **line plot** uses marks to show the number of times that each value or result occurs.

Example

In their last ten football seasons, the Tigers won 1, 6, 2, 5, 10, 6, 11, 10, 9, and 8 games. The following line plot shows the data.

Tigers

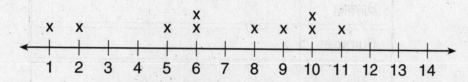

Number of Games Won in a Season

Each X on the line plot shows a season in which the Tigers won that number of games.

Practice

Directions: Use the line plot above to answer Numbers 1 through 4.

1. What is the least number of games that the Tigers won in a season?

_____

2. How many times did the Tigers win 8 games? _____

3. What is the most number of games that the Tigers won in a season?

_____

4. How many times did the Tigers win 6 games? _____

Directions: Ask each of the students in your class which season (winter, spring, summer, or fall) is his or her favorite. Then use the data to answer Numbers 5 through 8.

5. Fill in the following tally chart with your data.

Students' Favorite Season

Season	Number of Students	
Winter		
Spring		
Summer		
Fall		

6. Make a line plot of the data.

Students' Favorite Season

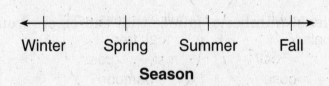

Winter   Spring   Summer   Fall

Season

7. How many students in your class said that spring is his or her favorite season?

_____

8. Write a sentence that compares the number of students in your class who said that winter is his or her favorite season to the number of students who said that summer is his or her favorite.

_____

_____

Venn Diagrams

Venn diagrams help you see the relationships between different sets. They show which objects the sets have in common and which objects are in only one set.

The objects that are grouped in a set will be within a circle. The label telling how the objects are grouped will be listed at the top of each circle.

Example

Jonathon was asked to group these objects into sets.

rabbit, tulip, seaweed, monkey, rose, grass, calf, bamboo, mouse, oak tree

Jonathon studied the objects and noticed that some were animals and some were plants. He decided to group these objects into two sets: animals and plants. Here are his sets.

Animals: rabbit, monkey, calf, mouse

Plants: tulip, seaweed, rose, grass, bamboo, oak tree

Here is the Venn diagram to show the two sets.

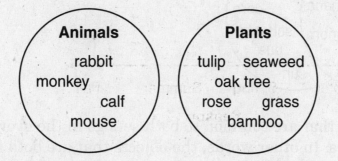

Notice that the circles do not overlap or touch. This means that the sets have no common objects between them. In other words, there are no animals that are also plants.

Sometimes the circles will overlap if there is an object that can be grouped within more than one set. Look at the next example.

 Example

Jonathon was asked to group these objects into sets.

apple, school bus, corn, banana, lemon, cherry, sun, lime

Jonathon looked at the objects and noticed that some of the objects were fruits and some were objects that are yellow. He decided to group the objects into two sets: fruits and yellow objects. Here are his sets.

Fruits: apple, **banana**, **lemon**, cherry, lime

Yellow Objects: school bus, corn, **banana**, **lemon**, sun

Notice that banana and lemon are in both sets. They are both fruits and yellow objects. Here is the Venn diagram to show two sets that have objects in common.

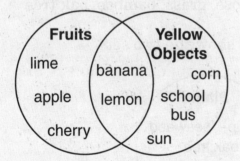

Only the objects that are common to both sets go in the overlapping part of the circles. In other words, the objects that are both fruits and yellow are inside both of the circles.

Practice

Directions: Use the Venn diagram to answer Numbers 1 through 3.

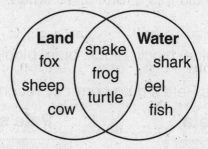

1. How many animals are shown that live on land? _____

2. How many animals are shown that live in water? _____

3. How many animals are shown that live both on land and in water?

_____

4. Draw a Venn diagram to show how the following numbers are grouped. Be sure to label your Venn diagram for each set.

Count by 2s: 2, 4, 6, 8, 10, 12, 14, 16, 18, 20

Count by 5s: 5, 10, 15, 20

Mathematics Practice

1. Pete picked a block out of a bag without looking, recorded the color, and put it back into the bag. He did this a total of 10 times. Here is a list of the colors that he picked:

    red, black, yellow, blue, black, black, blue, black, red, blue

    Which tally chart shows Pete's data correctly recorded?

Ⓐ **Pete's Block Data**

Outcome	Number Picked	
Blue	II	2
Red	IIII	4
Yellow	III	3
Black	I	1

Ⓒ **Pete's Block Data**

Outcome	Number Picked	
Blue	III	3
Red	II	2
Yellow	I	1
Black	IIII	4

Ⓑ **Pete's Block Data**

Outcome	Number Picked	
Blue	I	1
Red	II	2
Yellow	III	3
Black	IIII	4

Ⓓ **Pete's Block Data**

Outcome	Number Picked	
Blue	IIII	4
Red	I	1
Yellow	III	3
Black	II	2

2. Mike asked 10 of his friends what kinds of pets they had. The Venn diagram shows his results.

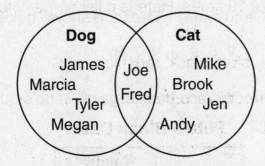

Who has only a cat for a pet?

Ⓐ Joe

Ⓑ Fred

Ⓒ James

Ⓓ Brook

3. The following bar graph shows the number of cars that Kim's Autos sold over 3 days.

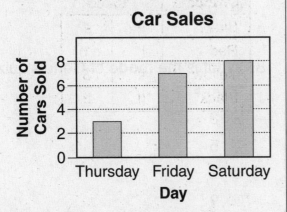

How many cars did Kim's Autos sell on Friday and Saturday combined?

Ⓐ 15

Ⓑ 11

Ⓒ 10

Ⓓ 8

4. Hazel took a survey of which roller coaster students liked the best. The results are shown in the pictograph.

Number of Students Who Liked Each Roller Coaster Best

Cyclone	☺☺☺☺☺☺
Vortex	☺☺☺☺☺☺☺☺
Thunder	☺☺☺
Goldrusher	☺☺☺☺☺☺☺

KEY
☺ = 2 students

How many more students liked Cyclone than Thunder?

Ⓐ 3

Ⓑ 4

Ⓒ 6

Ⓓ 9

5. Elsie asked each of her classmates what kind of pet he or she would like to own. Her results are shown in the bar graph.

Pets Elsie's Classmates Would Like to Own

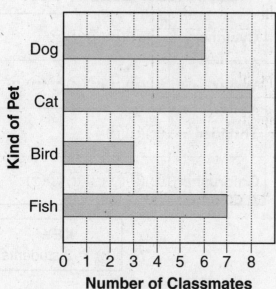

Which kind of pet did the **most** classmates say they would like to own?

Ⓐ dog

Ⓑ cat

Ⓒ bird

Ⓓ fish

Directions: Use the following information to answer Numbers 6 through 8.

Geno's quiz scores are shown below.

9, 5, 9, 3, 9, 7, 8

6. What is the **range** of Geno's quiz scores?

Ⓐ 6

Ⓑ 7

Ⓒ 8

Ⓓ 9

7. What is the **median** of Geno's quiz scores?

Ⓐ 9

Ⓑ 8

Ⓒ 7

Ⓓ 6

8. What is the **mode** of Geno's quiz scores?

Ⓐ 3

Ⓑ 5

Ⓒ 7

Ⓓ 9

9. Lexi wrote down the number of teeth that the students in her third-grade class have lost. The data she collected are found in the following tally chart.

Lost Teeth

Number of Teeth Lost	Number of Students	
3	|||	3
4	||||	4
5	⊞|||	8
6	⊞||	7

Part A
Make a line plot that correctly displays the data from the chart.

Part B
What is the mode of the number of teeth lost? _____

Lesson 16: Probability

Probability is the chance that something will happen.

Possible Outcomes

When you test the probability of an event happening, you perform a **probability experiment**. Every probability experiment has a number of **possible outcomes**.

Example

Shania will spin the spinner once. What are the possible outcomes when she spins the spinner?

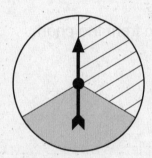

The possible outcomes when Shania spins the spinner are white, gray, and striped.

Practice

1. Travis will flip a quarter. What are the possible outcomes?

   _____

2. Marge will roll a number cube numbered 1 through 6. What are the possible outcomes?

   _____

Determining Likelihood

Most probability experiments have more than one outcome. Different outcomes have different probabilities. An outcome with the highest probability is **most likely** to occur. An outcome with a lowest probability is **least likely** to occur. Two outcomes are **equally likely** to occur if the probability of each outcome is the same.

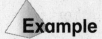 **Example**

Maria will pick one marble out of the bag without looking.

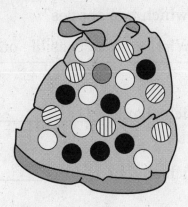

There are 7 white marbles, 6 black marbles, 6 striped marbles, and 1 gray marble.

There are more white marbles than any other color, so Maria is **most likely** to pick a white marble.

There are less gray marbles than any other color, so she is **least likely** to pick a gray marble.

There are the same number of black and striped marbles, so she is **equally likely** to pick a black marble or a striped marble.

Practice

Directions: Use the following spinner to answer Numbers 1 through 3.

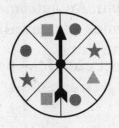

1. The arrow is **equally likely** to land on which two shapes?

    _____

2. The arrow is **most likely** to land on which shape? _____

3. The arrow is **least likely** to land on which shape? _____

Directions: Use the following spinner to answer Numbers 4 through 6.

4. The arrow is **equally likely** to land on which two numbers?

    _____

5. The arrow is **most likely** to land on which number? _____

6. The arrow is **least likely** to land on which number? _____

Certain and Impossible

An outcome that will always happen is **certain**. An outcome that will never happen is **impossible**.

 Example

David will pick one object out of the bag without looking. What is the probability he will pick a triangle?

David is **certain** to pick a triangle.

 Example

Marlon will spin the spinner 1 time. What is the probability the arrow will land on an octagon?

Since there are no octagons on the spinner, it is **impossible** for the arrow to land on an octagon.

Practice

Directions: For Numbers 1 through 3, tell whether each event is *certain* or *impossible*.

1. rolling a 7 on a number cube numbered 1 through 6 _____

2. scoring 105 on a test out of 100 points _____

3. rolling a number less than 7 on a number cube numbered 1 through 6

_____

Directions: Use the spinner below to answer Numbers 4 and 5. Tell whether each event is *certain* or *impossible*.

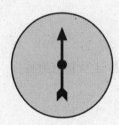

4. landing on a gray section _____

5. landing on a white section _____

Directions: Use the bag of marbles below to answer Numbers 6 and 7. Jessie will choose one marble from the bag without looking.

6. Name an event that is **impossible**. _____

7. Name an event that is **certain**. _____

Determining Probability

Successful outcomes are the number of ways in which the event you want can happen. **Total outcomes** are the number of ways in which all possible events can happen. If you are flipping a coin and want it to land heads up, there is one successful outcome (heads) and two total outcomes (heads and tails).

You can show the probability of an event happening as a fraction, as shown below.

$$\text{probability } (P) = \frac{\text{number of successful outcomes}}{\text{number of total outcomes}}$$

You can also describe the probability as the number of successful outcomes "out of" the number of total outcomes.

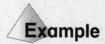

Example

These marbles are placed in a bag. If Tanya picks one without looking, what is the probability she will pick a white marble?

Since Tanya wants to get a white marble, and there are 3 white marbles in the bag, the number of successful outcomes is 3. There are 4 marbles in the bag, so the number of total outcomes is 4.

So, the probability of picking a white marble is $\frac{3}{4}$. In other words, the probability that Tanya will pick the white marble is 3 out of 4.

Practice

Directions: Use the following information to answer Numbers 1 through 3.

Veronica is going to pick a marble from this sack of marbles without looking.

1. What is the probability that Veronica will pick a ⬤? _____

2. What is the probability that Veronica will pick a ⬤? _____

3. What is the probability that Veronica will pick a ○? _____

4. Abby has 1 red, 2 yellow, 1 blue, and 4 green pencils inside her desk. She reaches in without looking and takes one out. What is the probability that the pencil is yellow?

   A. $\frac{1}{2}$

   B. $\frac{2}{4}$

   C. $\frac{2}{8}$

   D. $\frac{6}{8}$

5. There are 20 students in your class. Your teacher places one piece of paper with each student's name in a hat and then draws one name from the hat. What is the probability that your teacher will pick your name?

   A. 1 out of 5

   B. 1 out of 10

   C. 1 out of 20

   D. 2 out of 100

Experiments

You can guess the results of a probability experiment by looking at all of the possible outcomes. After you look at all of the possible outcomes, you can do the experiment and record the results that you get by making a list or table.

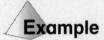 **Example**

Kwami looked at all of the possible outcomes of a probability experiment in which he will spin the following spinner.

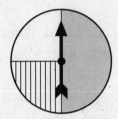

Kwami knew that the possible outcomes were gray (G), white (W), and striped (S).

He also knew that the arrow was more likely to land on the gray section than on the white section or the striped section. Kwami also recognized that the arrow was equally likely to land on the white section and the striped section.

Kwami spun the spinner 8 times and recorded his results in the table below.

Spin number	1	2	3	4	5	6	7	8
Outcome	S	G	G	W	W	G	G	G

In Kwami's experiment, the arrow landed on the gray section 5 times, the white section 2 times, and the striped section 1 time.

Practice

Directions: For Numbers 1 through 5, you will be doing a probability experiment. In the experiment, you will flip a coin ten times and record the outcomes in a table.

1. When you flip a coin, what are the possible outcomes?

   _____

2. Are there any outcomes that are more likely to occur than others? Are there any outcomes that are less likely to occur than others?

   _____

   _____

3. Flip the coin ten times. Write down the outcomes in the following table. Use H for heads and T for tails.

Coin flip	1	2	3	4	5	6	7	8	9	10
Outcome										

4. Now do the experiment again. Write the outcomes in the following table. Again, use H for heads and T for tails.

Coin flip	1	2	3	4	5	6	7	8	9	10
Outcome										

5. How close were the results of your second experiment to the results of your first experiment?

   _____

   _____

Mathematics Practice

Directions: Use the following information to answer Numbers 1 and 2.

Rob will pick a marble out of the following bag without looking.

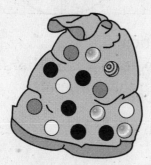

1. Which type of marble is Rob **least likely** to pick?

   Ⓐ ⬤ (gray)

   Ⓑ ⬤ (light gray)

   Ⓒ ⬤ (black)

   Ⓓ ◎ (swirl)

2. Rob is **equally likely** to pick which two types of marbles?

   Ⓐ ◯ and ◎

   Ⓑ ⬤ and ⬤

   Ⓒ ◯ and ⬤

   Ⓓ ⬤ and ◎

3. At a birthday party, each person gets to spin the arrow on the spinner once to see what prize he or she will win.

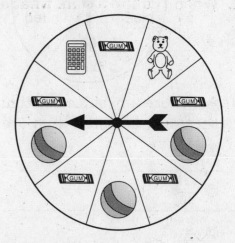

   What prize is **most likely** to be won?

   Ⓐ pack of gum

   Ⓑ teddy bear

   Ⓒ ball

   Ⓓ calculator

4. William is going to pick a number from 1 to 10. What is the probability that William will pick the number 6?

   Ⓐ $\frac{1}{10}$

   Ⓑ $\frac{2}{10}$

   Ⓒ $\frac{4}{10}$

   Ⓓ $\frac{6}{10}$

5. What is the probability of the spinner landing on blue?

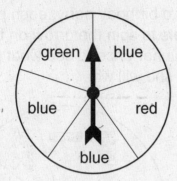

Ⓐ $\frac{1}{10}$

Ⓑ $\frac{1}{5}$

Ⓒ $\frac{5}{10}$

Ⓓ $\frac{3}{5}$

6. Mary has a box of green pens. She is going to pick a pen without looking. Which describes the probability of Mary picking a green pen?

Ⓐ equally likely

Ⓑ most likely

Ⓒ certain

Ⓓ impossible

7. Which describes the probability of the spinner landing on yellow?

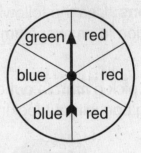

Ⓐ certain

Ⓑ impossible

Ⓒ most likely

Ⓓ equally likely

8. Jennie labeled the sides of a cube with the letters of her name. If she rolls the cube 1 time, what is the probability the letter E will land up?

Ⓐ $\frac{2}{6}$

Ⓑ $\frac{2}{4}$

Ⓒ $\frac{1}{4}$

Ⓓ $\frac{1}{2}$